Treating Tobacco Use and Dependence

Guideline Panel

Michael C. Fiore, MD (Panel Chair)
William C. Bailey, MD
Stuart J. Cohen, EdD
Sally Faith Dorfman, MD, MSHSA
Michael G. Goldstein, MD
Ellen R. Gritz, PhD
Richard B. Heyman, MD
Carlos Roberto Jaén, MD, PhD
Thomas E. Kottke, MD, MSPH
Harry A. Lando, PhD
Robert E. Mecklenburg, DDS, MPH
Patricia Dolan Mullen, DrPH
Louise M. Nett, RN, RRT
Lawrence Robinson, MD, MPH
Maxine L. Stitzer, PhD
Anthony C. Tommasello, MS
Louise Villejo, MPH, CHES
Mary Ellen Wewers, PhD, RN

Guideline Staff

Timothy Baker, PhD
Brion J. Fox, JD
Victor Hasselblad, PhD

U.S. Department of Health and Human Services
Public Health Service
June 2000

Guideline Development and Use

Treating Tobacco Use and Dependence, a Public Health Service-sponsored Clinical Practice Guideline, is the result of an extraordinary partnership among Federal Government and nonprofit organizations comprised of the Agency for Healthcare Research and Quality; Centers for Disease Control and Prevention; National Cancer Institute; National Heart, Lung, and Blood Institute; National Institute on Drug Abuse; Robert Wood Johnson Foundation; and University of Wisconsin Medical School's Center for Tobacco Research and Intervention. Each member of this consortium is dedicated to improving the Nation's public health, and their participation in this collaboration clearly demonstrates a strong commitment to tobacco cessation.

This guideline is an updated version of the 1996 *Smoking Cessation Clinical Practice Guideline No. 18*. It is the product of a private-sector panel of experts, consortium representatives, and staff. The update was written to include new, effective clinical treatments for tobacco dependence that have become available since the original guideline was developed. *Treating Tobacco Use and Dependence* will make an important contribution to the quality of care in the United States and the health of the American people.

The panel employed an explicit, science-based methodology and expert clinical judgment to develop recommendations on the treatment of tobacco use and dependence. Extensive literature searches were conducted, and critical reviews and syntheses were used to evaluate empirical evidence and significant outcomes. Peer and field reviews were undertaken to evaluate the validity, reliability, and utility of the guideline in clinical practice. The panel's recommendations are primarily based on published, evidence-based research. When the evidence was incomplete or inconsistent in a particular area, the recommendations reflect the professional judgment of panel members and consultants.

The recommendations herein may not be appropriate for use in all circumstances. Decisions to adopt any particular recommendation must be made by clinicians in light of available resources and circumstances presented by individual patients.

This Public Health Service-sponsored Clinical Practice Guideline gives hope to the 7 out of 10 smokers who try to quit each year. I urge every clinician, health plan, and health care institution to make treating tobacco dependence a top priority. Please ask your patients two key questions: "Do you smoke?" "Do you want to quit?" followed by use of the recommendations in this guideline.

David Satcher, MD, PhD
U.S. Surgeon General
Assistant Secretary for Health

Abstract

Treating Tobacco Use and Dependence, a Public Health Service-sponsored Clinical Practice Guideline, is a product of the Tobacco Use and Dependence Guideline Panel ("the panel"), consortium representatives, consultants, and staff. These 30 individuals were charged with the responsibility of identifying effective, experimentally validated tobacco dependence treatments and practices. The updated guideline was sponsored by a consortium of seven Federal Government and nonprofit organizations: the Agency for Healthcare Research and Quality (AHRQ); Centers for Disease Control and Prevention (CDC); National Cancer Institute (NCI); National Heart, Lung, and Blood Institute (NHLBI); National Institute on Drug Abuse (NIDA); Robert Wood Johnson Foundation (RWJF); and University of Wisconsin Medical School's Center for Tobacco Research and Intervention (CTRI). This guideline is an updated version of the 1996 *Smoking Cessation Clinical Practice Guideline No. 18* that was sponsored by the Agency for Health Care Policy and Research (now the AHRQ), U.S. Department of Health and Human Services. The original guideline reflected the extant scientific research literature published between 1975 and 1994.

The updated guideline was written because new, effective clinical treatments for tobacco dependence have been identified since 1994. The accelerating pace of tobacco research that prompted the update is reflected in the fact that 3,000 articles on tobacco were identified as published between 1975 and 1994, contributing to the original guideline. Another 3,000 were published between 1995 and 1999 and contributed to the updated guideline. These 6,000 articles were screened and reviewed to identify a much smaller group of articles that served as the basis for guideline data analyses and panel opinion.

This guideline contains strategies and recommendations designed to assist clinicians; tobacco dependence treatment specialists; and health care administrators, insurers, and purchasers in delivering and supporting effective treatments for tobacco use and dependence. The recommendations were made as a result of a systematic review and analysis of the extant scientific literature, using meta-analysis as the primary analytic technique. The strength of evidence that served as the basis for each recommendation is clearly indicated in the guideline. A draft of the guideline was peer-reviewed prior to publication, and the comments of 70 external reviewers were incorporated into the final document. The key recommendations of the updated guideline, *Treating Tobacco Use and Dependence,* based on the literature review and expert panel opinion, are as follows:

1. Tobacco dependence is a chronic condition that often requires repeated intervention. However, effective treatments exist that can produce long-term or even permanent abstinence.

2. Because effective tobacco dependence treatments are available, every patient who uses tobacco should be offered at least one of these treatments:

- Patients *willing* to try to quit tobacco use should be provided with treatments identified as effective in this guideline.

- Patients *unwilling* to try to quit tobacco use should be provided with a brief intervention designed to increase their motivation to quit.

3. It is essential that clinicians and health care delivery systems (including administrators, insurers, and purchasers) institutionalize the consistent identification, documentation, and treatment of every tobacco user seen in a health care setting.

4. Brief tobacco dependence treatment is effective, and every patient who uses tobacco should be offered at least brief treatment.

5. There is a strong dose-response relation between the intensity of tobacco dependence counseling and its effectiveness. Treatments involving person-to-person contact (via individual, group, or proactive telephone counseling) are consistently effective, and their effectiveness increases with treatment intensity (e.g., minutes of contact).

6. Three types of counseling and behavioral therapies were found to be especially effective and should be used with all patients attempting tobacco cessation:

- Provision of practical counseling (problemsolving/skills training);

- Provision of social support as part of treatment (intra-treatment social support); and

- Help in securing social support outside of treatment (extra-treatment social support).

7. Numerous effective pharmacotherapies for smoking cessation now exist. Except in the presence of contraindications, these should be used with all patients attempting to quit smoking.

- Five *first-line* pharmacotherapies were identified that reliably increase long-term smoking abstinence rates:
  – Bupropion SR
  – Nicotine gum
  – Nicotine inhaler
  – Nicotine nasal spray
  – Nicotine patch

- Two *second-line* pharmacotherapies were identified as efficacious and may be considered by clinicians if first-line pharmacotherapies are not effective:
  – Clonidine
  – Nortriptyline

- Over-the-counter nicotine patches are effective relative to placebo, and their use should be encouraged.

8. Tobacco dependence treatments are both clinically effective and cost-effective relative to other medical and disease prevention interventions. As such, insurers and purchasers should ensure that:

    - All insurance plans include as a reimbursed benefit the counseling and pharmacotherapeutic treatments identified as effective in this guideline; and

    - Clinicians are reimbursed for providing tobacco dependence treatment just as they are reimbursed for treating other chronic conditions.

The updated guideline is divided into eight chapters that provide an overview including methods (Chapter 1), information on the assessment of tobacco use (Chapter 2), brief clinical interventions, both for patients willing and unwilling to make a quit attempt at this time (Chapter 3), intensive clinical interventions (Chapter 4), systems interventions for health care administrators, insurers, and purchasers (Chapter 5), the scientific evidence supporting the guideline recommendations (Chapter 6), and special populations and topics (Chapters 7 and 8).

A comparison of the findings of the updated guideline with the original guideline reveals the considerable progress made in tobacco research over the brief period separating these two publications. Tobacco dependence is now increasingly recognized as a chronic disease, one that typically requires ongoing assessment and repeated intervention. In addition, the updated guideline offers the clinician many more efficacious treatment strategies than were identified in the original guideline. There are now seven different efficacious agents in the smoking cessation pharmacopoeia, allowing the clinician and patient many different medication options. In addition, recent evidence has identified new, efficacious counseling strategies. In particular, proactive telephone counseling is efficacious, as is counseling that helps smokers attain social support outside of the treatment context. The updated guideline also reveals greater evidence of the strong dose-response relation between counseling intensity and the likelihood of long-term abstinence from tobacco. Indeed, the data are compelling that pharmacologic and counseling treatment each independently boost cessation success; these data suggest that optimal cessation outcomes may require the combined use of both counseling and pharmacotherapy.

Finally, there is increasing evidence that the success of any tobacco dependence treatment strategy or effort cannot be divorced from the health care system in which it is embedded. Data strongly indicate that effective tobacco interventions require *coordinated interventions*. Just as the clinician must intervene with his or her patient, so must the health care administrator, insurer, and purchaser foster and support tobacco intervention as an integral element of health care delivery. Health care administrators and insurers should ensure that clinicians have the training and support, and receive the reimbursement necessary to achieve consistent, effective intervention with tobacco users.

One important conclusion of this guideline is that the most effective way to move clinicians to intervene is to provide them with information regarding multiple efficacious treatment options and to ensure that they have ample institutional support to use these options. Indeed, in this guideline, the panel encourages a culture of health care in which failure to treat tobacco use—the chief cause of preventable disease and death—constitutes an inappropriate standard of care.

Fiore MC, Bailey WC, Cohen SJ, et al. *Treating Tobacco Use and Dependence.* Clinical Practice Guideline. Rockville, MD: U.S. Department of Health and Human Services. Public Health Service. June 2000.

Acknowledgments

This guideline would not have been possible without the collaborative efforts of many individuals and organizations. Each made significant contributions throughout the process of updating this guideline. While too numerous to list here, the Contributors section of this publication provides a listing of support staff, individual peer reviewers, and others. There are, however, some individuals and organizations that deserve special mention.

The panel wishes to acknowledge the support and guidance provided by the consortium partners in general and their dedicated, hard working representatives in particular. Specifically, the panel gratefully acknowledges the extraordinarily supportive efforts and substantial contribution throughout the project of Ernestine W. Murray, RN, MAS, Panel Project Officer, Center for Practice and Technology Assessment, Agency for Healthcare Research and Quality (AHRQ). Additionally, we would like to recognize the outstanding contributions of other AHRQ staff: Douglas B. Kamerow, MD, MPH, Director, Center for Practice and Technology Assessment; Harriett V. Bennett, Public Affairs and Marketing Specialist, Office of Health Care Information; and Sandra Katz Cummings, Managing Editor, Office of Health Care Information. The panel particularly wishes to thank Glen D. Morgan, PhD, at the National Cancer Institute; Corinne Husten, MD, MPH, and Cathy Melvin, PhD, MPH, Office on Smoking and Health at the Centers for Disease Control and Prevention; Glen Bennett, MPH, at the National Heart, Lung, and Blood Institute; Stephen J. Heishman, PhD, at the National Institute on Drug Abuse; C. Tracy Orleans, PhD, at the Robert Wood Johnson Foundation; and Douglas Jorenby, PhD, at the Center for Tobacco Research and Intervention, University of Wisconsin Medical School.

The panel also wishes to thank Marc Manley, MD, MPH; John Mullahy, PhD; David Schriger, MD, MPH; and David Wetter, PhD, consultants on the project, for their insight and intellectual contributions.

Finally, the panel extends its gratitude and appreciation to the staff members at the University of Wisconsin Medical School's Center for Tobacco Research and Intervention for their tireless efforts in bringing this project to completion. In particular, the panel acknowledges and thanks Bridget Whisler, Project Manager; and Megan Piper, MA, and Sam Welsch, Senior Research Associates.

Contents

Strategies

Figures

Executive Summary

Context

In America today, tobacco stands out as the agent most responsible for avoidable illness and death. Millions of Americans consume this toxin on a daily basis. Its use brings premature death to almost half a million Americans each year, and it contributes to profound disability and pain in many others. Approximately one-third of all tobacco users in this country will die prematurely because of their dependence on tobacco. Unlike so many epidemics in the past, there is a clear, contemporaneous understanding of the cause of this premature death and disability—the use of tobacco. It is a testament to the power of tobacco addiction that millions of tobacco users have been unable to overcome their dependence and save themselves from its consequences: perpetual worry, unceasing expense, and compromised health. Indeed, it is difficult to identify any other condition that presents such a mix of lethality, prevalence, and neglect, despite effective and readily available interventions.

Despite high, sustained tobacco use prevalence, the response of both clinicians and the U.S. health care delivery system is disappointing. Studies show that most smokers present at primary care settings, and they are not offered effective assistance in quitting. The smoker's lack of success in quitting, and the clinician's reluctance to intervene, can be traced to many factors. Until recently, few effective treatments existed, effective treatments had not been identified clearly, and health care systems had not supported their consistent and universal delivery. To single-out the clinician for blame would be inappropriate, when he or she has typically received neither the training nor support necessary to treat tobacco use successfully.

Current treatments for tobacco dependence offer clinicians their greatest single opportunity to staunch the loss of life, health, and happiness caused by this chronic condition. It is imperative, therefore, that clinicians actively assess and treat tobacco use. In addition, it is imperative that health care administrators, insurers, and purchasers adopt and support policies and practices that are aimed at reducing tobacco use prevalence. The chief purpose of this document is to provide clinicians, tobacco dependence specialists, health care administrators, insurers, and purchasers, and even tobacco users, with evidence-based recommendations regarding clinical and systems interventions that will increase the likelihood of successful quitting.

Guideline Origins

This updated guideline, *Treating Tobacco Use and Dependence,* a Public Health Service-sponsored Clinical Practice Guideline, is the product of the Tobacco Use and Dependence Guideline Panel ("the panel"), consortium representatives, consultants, and staff. These 30 individuals were charged with the responsibility of identifying effective, experimentally validated, tobacco dependence treatments and practices. This guideline is an update of the 1996 *Smoking Cessation Clinical Practice Guideline No. 18* that was sponsored by the Agency for Health Care Policy and Research (now the Agency for Healthcare Research and Quality [AHRQ]), U.S. Department of Health and Human Services. The original guideline reflected the extant scientific research literature published between 1975 and 1994.

The updated guideline was written in response to new, effective clinical treatments for tobacco dependence that have been identified since 1994, and that these treatments promise to enhance the rates of successful tobacco cessation. The accelerating pace of tobacco research that prompted the update is reflected by the fact that 3,000 articles on tobacco published between 1975 and 1994 were collected and screened as part of the original guideline. Another 3,000 were published between 1995 and 1999 and contributed to the updated guideline. These 6,000 articles were reviewed to identify a much smaller group of articles that served as the basis for guideline data analyses and panel opinion.

The updated guideline was sponsored by a consortium of seven Federal Government and nonprofit organizations: the Agency for Healthcare Research and Quality (AHRQ); Centers for Disease Control and Prevention (CDC); National Cancer Institute (NCI); National Heart, Lung, and Blood Institute (NHLBI); National Institute on Drug Abuse (NIDA); Robert Wood Johnson Foundation (RWJF); and University of Wisconsin Medical School's Center for Tobacco Research and Intervention (CTRI). All of these organizations have the mission to reduce the human costs of tobacco use. Given the importance of this issue to the health of all Americans, the updated guideline is published by the U.S. Public Health Service.

Guideline Style and Structure

This guideline was written to be relevant to all tobacco users—those using cigarettes as well as other forms of tobacco. Therefore, the terms "tobacco user" and "tobacco dependence" will be used in preference to "smoker" and "cigarette dependence." However, in some cases the evidence for a particular recommendation consists entirely of studies using smokers as subjects. In these instances, the recommendation and evidence refers to "smoking" to communicate the parochial nature of the evidence. In most cases though, guideline recommendations are relevant to all types of tobacco users.

The updated guideline is divided into eight chapters:

Chapter 1, Overview and Methods, provides the clinical practice and scientific context of the guideline update project and describes the methodology used to generate the guideline findings.

Chapter 2, Assessment of Tobacco Use, describes how each patient presenting at a health care setting should have his or her tobacco use status determined, and how tobacco users should be assessed for willingness to make a quit attempt.

Chapter 3, Brief Clinical Interventions, summarizes effective brief interventions that can easily be delivered in a primary care setting. In this chapter, separate interventions are described for the patient who is *willing* to try to quit at this time, for the patient who is *not yet willing* to try to quit, and for the patient who has recently quit.

Chapter 4, Intensive Clinical Interventions, outlines a prototype of an intensive tobacco cessation treatment that comprises strategies shown to be effective in this guideline. Because intensive treatments produce the highest success rates, they are an important element in tobacco intervention strategies.

Chapter 5, Systems Interventions: Relevance to Health Care Administrators, Insurers, and Purchasers, offers a blueprint to guideline changes in health care coverage and health care administration such that tobacco assessment and intervention become "default options" in health care delivery.

Chapter 6, Evidence, presents the results of guideline statistical analyses and the recommendations that emanate from them. Guideline analyses address topics such as the efficacy of different pharmacotherapies and counseling strategies, the relation between treatment intensities and treatment success, and whether screening for tobacco use in the clinic setting enhances tobacco user identification. The guideline panel made specific recommendations regarding future research on these topics.

Chapter 7, Special Populations, evaluates evidence on tobacco intervention strategies and efficacy with special populations (e.g., women, pregnant smokers, racial and ethnic minorities, hospitalized smokers, smokers with psychiatric comorbidity and chemical dependency, children and adolescents, and older smokers). The guideline panel made specific recommendations for future research on topics relevant to these populations.

Chapter 8, Special Topics, presents information and recommendations relevant to weight gain after smoking cessation, noncigarette tobacco products, clinician training, economics of tobacco treatment, and harm reduction. The guideline panel formulated specific recommendations regarding future research on these topics.

Findings and Recommendations

The key recommendations of the updated guideline, *Treating Tobacco Use and Dependence*, based on the literature review and expert panel opinion, are as follows:

1. Tobacco dependence is a chronic condition that often requires repeated intervention. However, effective treatments exist that can produce long-term or even permanent abstinence.

2. Because effective tobacco dependence treatments are available, every patient who uses tobacco should be offered at least one of these treatments:

   - Patients *willing* to try to quit tobacco use should be provided treatments identified as effective in this guideline.

   - Patients *unwilling* to try to quit tobacco use should be provided a brief intervention designed to increase their motivation to quit.

3. It is essential that clinicians and health care delivery systems (including administrators, insurers, and purchasers) institutionalize the consistent identification, documentation, and treatment of every tobacco user seen in a health care setting.

4. Brief tobacco dependence treatment is effective, and every patient who uses tobacco should be offered at least brief treatment.

5. There is a strong dose-response relation between the intensity of tobacco dependence counseling and its effectiveness. Treatments involving person-to-person contact (via individual, group, or proactive telephone counseling) are consistently effective, and their effectiveness increases with treatment intensity (e.g., minutes of contact).

6. Three types of counseling and behavioral therapies were found to be especially effective and should be used with all patients attempting tobacco cessation:

   - Provision of practical counseling (problemsolving/skills training);

   - Provision of social support as part of treatment (intra-treatment social support); and

   - Help in securing social support outside of treatment (extra-treatment social support).

7. Numerous effective pharmacotherapies for smoking cessation now exist. Except in the presence of contraindications, these should be used with all patients attempting to quit smoking.

   - Five *first-line* pharmacotherapies were identified that reliably increase long-term smoking abstinence rates:
     - Bupropion SR
     - Nicotine gum
     - Nicotine inhaler
     - Nicotine nasal spray
     - Nicotine patch

   - Two *second-line* pharmacotherapies were identified as efficacious and may be considered by clinicians if first-line pharmacotherapies are not effective:
     - Clonidine
     - Nortriptyline

   - Over-the-counter nicotine patches are effective relative to placebo, and their use should be encouraged.

8. Tobacco dependence treatments are both clinically effective and cost-effective relative to other medical and disease prevention interventions. As such, insurers and purchasers should ensure that:

- All insurance plans include as a reimbursed benefit the counseling and pharmacotherapeutic treatments identified as effective in this guideline; and

- Clinicians are reimbursed for providing tobacco dependence treatment just as they are reimbursed for treating other chronic conditions.

Guideline Update: Advances

A comparison of the findings of the year 2000 guideline with the previous 1996 guideline reveals the considerable progress made in tobacco research over the brief period separating these two works. Among many important differences between the two documents, the following deserve special note:

- The updated guideline has produced even stronger evidence of the association between counseling intensity and successful treatment outcomes, and also has revealed evidence of additional efficacious counseling strategies. These include telephone counseling and counseling that helps smokers enlist support outside the treatment context.

- The updated guideline offers the clinician many more efficacious pharmaco-logic treatment strategies than were identified in the previous guideline. There are now seven different efficacious smoking cessation medications, allowing the clinician and patient many more treatment options. Further information also is available on the efficacy of combinations of nicotine replacement therapies and pharmacotherapies that are obtained over-the-counter.

- The updated guideline contains strong evidence that smoking cessation treatments shown to be efficacious in this guideline (both pharmacotherapy and counseling) are *cost-effective* relative to other routinely reimbursed medical interventions (e.g., treatment of hyperlipidemia and mammography screening). The guideline panel concluded, therefore, that smoking cessation treatments should not be withheld from patients given the fact that they are both cost-effective and clinically effective.

Coordination of Care: Institutionalizing the Treatment of Tobacco Dependence

There is increasing evidence that the success of any tobacco dependence treatment strategy cannot be divorced from the health care system in which it is embedded. Data strongly indicate that the consistent and effective delivery of tobacco interventions requires *coordinated interventions*. Just as a clinician must intervene with his or her patient, so must the health care administrator, insurer, and purchaser foster and support tobacco dependence treatment as an integral element of health care delivery. Health care purchasers should demand that tobacco intervention be a contractually covered obligation of insurers and providers. Health care administrators and insurers should ensure that clinicians have the training and support, and receive the reimbursement necessary to achieve consistent, effective intervention with tobacco users.

Future Promise

About 20 years ago, data indicated that clinicians too frequently failed to intervene with their patients who smoke. Recent data confirm that this picture has not changed markedly over the past two decades. One recent study reported that only 15 percent of smokers who saw a physician in the past year were offered assistance with quitting, and only 3 percent were given a followup appointment to address this topic. These data are disheartening. The updated guideline reports a family of findings that creates tremendous tension for change. This guideline reveals that multiple efficacious treatments exist, these treatments can double or triple the likelihood of long-term cessation, many cessation treatments are appropriate for the primary care setting, cessation treatments are more cost-effective than many other reimbursed clinical interventions, and the utilization and impact of cessation treatments can be increased by supportive health system policies (e.g., coverage through insurance plans). In sum, the updated guideline identifies and describes scientifically validated treatments and offers clear guidance on how such treatments can be consistently and effectively integrated into health care delivery.

The guideline panel is optimistic that this updated guideline is a harbinger of a new and very promising era in the treatment of tobacco use and dependence. The guideline codifies an evolving culture of health care—one in which every tobacco user has access to effective treatments for tobacco dependence. This new standard of care provides clinicians and health care delivery systems with their greatest opportunity to improve the current and future health of their patients by assisting those addicted to tobacco. Tobacco users and their families deserve no less.

1 Overview and Methods

Introduction

Tobacco use has been cited as the chief avoidable cause of illness and death in our society, responsible for more than 430,000 deaths in the United States each year.[1] Smoking is a known cause of cancer, heart disease, stroke, complications of pregnancy, and chronic obstructive pulmonary disease.[2] Given the health dangers it presents and the public's awareness of those dangers, tobacco use remains surprisingly prevalent. Recent estimates are that 25 percent of adult Americans smoke.[3,4,5] Moreover, smoking prevalence among adolescents has risen dramatically since 1990,[6] with more than 3,000 additional children and adolescents becoming regular users of tobacco each day.[7,8] As a result, a new generation of Americans has become dependent upon tobacco and is at risk for the extraordinarily harmful consequences of tobacco use.

Tobacco use is not only dangerous to individuals, it also results in staggering societal costs. The estimated smoking-attributable cost for medical care in 1993 was more than $50 billion,[9] and the cost of lost productivity and forfeited earnings due to smoking-related disability was estimated at $47 billion per year.[10]

Despite the tragic health consequences of using tobacco, clinicians often fail to assess and treat tobacco use consistently and effectively. For instance, in 1995 smoking status was identified in only about 67 percent of clinic visits, and smoking cessation counseling was provided in only 21 percent of smokers' clinic visits.[11] Moreover, treatment is typically offered only to patients already suffering from tobacco-related diseases.[11] This failure to assess and intervene consistently with tobacco users exists in the face of substantial evidence that even brief smoking cessation treatments can be effective.[12-15]

This guideline concludes that tobacco use presents a rare confluence of circumstances: (1) a highly significant health threat; (2) a disinclination among clinicians to intervene consistently; and (3) the presence of effective interventions. This last point is buttressed by evidence that smoking cessation interventions, if delivered in a timely and effective manner, significantly reduce the smoker's risk of suffering from smoking-related disease.[16,17] Indeed, it is difficult to identify any other condition that presents such a mix of lethality, prevalence, and neglect, despite effective and readily available interventions.

Finally, significant barriers exist that interfere with clinicians' assessment and treatment of smokers. Many clinicians lack knowledge about how to identify smokers quickly and easily, which treatments are efficacious, how such treatments can be delivered, and the relative efficacies of different treatments.[18] Additionally, they may fail to intervene because of inadequate clinic or institutional support for routine assessment and treatment of tobacco use[11,19,20] and for other reasons such as time constraints.[21,22]

Rationale for Initial Guideline Development and Year 2000 Update

In the early 1990s, the Agency for Health Care Research and Policy (now the Agency for Healthcare Research and Quality [AHRQ]) convened an expert panel to develop the *Smoking Cessation Clinical Practice Guideline No. 18* (the "guideline") in the AHCPR series of Clinical Practice Guidelines. The need for this guideline was based on several factors, including tobacco use prevalence, related morbidity and mortality, the economic burden imposed by tobacco use, variation in clinical practice, availability of methods for improvement of care, and availability of data upon which to base recommendations for care.

Since the guideline was published in 1996, it has become a popular document. More than 1 million copies of the guideline and its affiliated products have been disseminated. Guideline recommendations have inspired changes in diverse health care settings such as health maintenance organizations and Veteran's Administration hospitals. The original guideline continues to provide a framework for educating clinicians, administrators, and policymakers about the importance of tobacco dependence and its treatment. It has stimulated discussions that address the development of tobacco dependence treatment programs at the Federal and State levels and by professional medical organizations.

Significant new research on tobacco use and its treatment has appeared since the publication of the original guideline. As a result of this new research, as well as an increasing recognition that tobacco interventions must become an integral part of health care delivery, the expert panel that developed the 1996 *Smoking Cessation Clinical Practice Guideline No. 18* was reconvened in 1998 to conduct an update. This guideline update is sponsored by a consortium of private and public partners, including the AHRQ; National Cancer Institute (NCI); National Heart, Lung, and Blood Institute (NHLBI); National Institute on Drug Abuse (NIDA); Office on Smoking and Health at the Centers for Disease Control and Prevention (CDC); Robert Wood Johnson Foundation (RWJF); and University of Wisconsin Medical School's Center for Tobacco Research and Intervention (CTRI).

The original guideline addressed barriers to effective smoking cessation intervention on the basis of a careful evaluation and synthesis of relevant scientific evidence. The guideline comprised specific evidence-based recommendations to guide clinicians and smoking cessation specialists in their tobacco intervention efforts. Additional specific recommendations guided insurers, purchasers, and health care administrators in their efforts to develop and implement institutional and policy changes that support the reliable assessment and treatment of tobacco dependence.

The updated guideline, *Treating Tobacco Use and Dependence,* a Public Health Service-sponsored Clinical Practice Guideline, provides recommendations based on evidence published through January 1, 1999. This new title underscores three truths about tobacco use.[23] First, all tobacco products, not just cigarettes, exact devastating costs on the Nation's health and welfare. Second, for most users, tobacco use results in true drug dependence, one comparable to the dependence caused by opiates, amphetamines, and cocaine.[24] Third, chronic tobacco use warrants clinical intervention just as do other addictive disorders.[18,25]

Most tobacco users in the United States are cigarette smokers. As a result, the majority of clinician attention and research in the field has focused on the treatment and assessment of smoking. However, clinicians should intervene with all tobacco users, not just with smokers. To foster a broad implementation of this guideline, every effort has been made to describe interventions so that they are relevant to all forms of tobacco use. In some sections of this guideline (e.g., sections of Chapter 6), the term "smoker" is used instead of "tobacco user." The use of the term "smoker" merely means that all relevant evidence for a recommendation arises exclusively from studies of cigarette smokers. Additional discussion of noncigarette forms of tobacco use is found in Chapter 8.

It is important to note that other guidelines and analyses on the treatment of tobacco dependence have been published, including those from the American Psychiatric Association,[26] the American Medical Association,[27] the United Kingdom Guideline,[28] and those published by the Cochrane Collaboration.[29]

Tobacco Dependence as a Chronic Disease

Tobacco dependence shows many features of a chronic disease. Although a minority of tobacco users achieves permanent abstinence in an initial quit attempt, the majority persist in tobacco use for many years and typically cycle through multiple periods of relapse and remission. A failure to appreciate the chronic nature of tobacco dependence may undercut clinicians' motivation to treat tobacco use consistently.

Epidemiologic data suggest that more than 70 percent of the 50 million smokers in the United States today have made at least one prior quit attempt, and approximately 46 percent try to quit each year.[4] Unfortunately, most of these efforts are unsuccessful; among the 17 million adults who attempted cessation in 1991, only about 7 percent were still abstinent 1 year later.[30,31] These discouraging statistics have led many clinicians to report that they feel ineffective in the treatment of tobacco dependence.

Moreover, as described in a recent editorial,[32] much smoking cessation research and clinical practice over the last three decades has focused on identifying the ideal intervention that would turn all smokers into permanent nonsmokers. This effort may have inadvertently communicated two messages of dubious validity: first, that there is one treatment that will be effective for virtually all smokers; and second, that success should be defined only on the basis of permanent abstinence. These messages may have masked the true nature of tobacco addiction; it is typically a chronic disorder that carries with it a vulnerability to relapse that persists for weeks, months, and perhaps years.

A more productive approach is to recognize the chronicity of tobacco dependence. A chronic disease model has many appealing aspects. It recognizes the long-term nature of the disorder with an expectation that patients may have periods of relapse and remission. If tobacco dependence is recognized as a chronic condition, clinicians will better understand the relapsing nature of the ailment and the requirement for ongoing, rather than just acute, care. Clinicians also should recognize that despite the potential for relapse, numerous effective treatments are now available and described in this guideline.

A chronic disease model emphasizes for clinicians the importance of counseling and advice. Although most clinicians are comfortable in counseling their patients about diabetes, hypertension, or hyperlipidemia, many believe that they are ineffective in providing counseling to patients who use tobacco. As with these chronic disorders, clinicians encountering a patient dependent on tobacco must be encouraged to provide that patient with simple counseling advice, support, and appropriate pharmacotherapy. In updating the guideline, the panel has presented evidence-based analytic findings in a format accessible and familiar to practicing clinicians. Although this should aid clinicians in the assessment and treatment of tobacco users, clinicians should remain cognizant that relapse is likely, and that it reflects the chronic nature of dependence, not their personal failure, nor a failure of their patients.

Guideline Development Methodology

Introduction

Panel recommendations are intended to provide clinicians with effective strategies for treating patients who use tobacco. Recommendations were influenced by two goals. The first was to identify clearly efficacious treatment strategies. The second was to formulate and present recommendations so that they can be implemented easily across diverse clinical settings and patient populations.

The guideline is based on two systematic reviews of the available scientific literature. The first review occurred during the creation of the original guideline published in 1996 and included literature published from 1975 through 1994. The second review was conducted for the updated guideline and included literature from 1995 through January 1, 1999. The two reviews were then combined into a single database.

The panel identified randomized placebo/comparison controlled trials as the strongest level of evidence for evaluation of treatment efficacy. Thus, evidence derived from randomized controlled trials serves as the basis for meta-analyses and for almost all recommendations contained in this guideline. However, the panel occasionally made recommendations in the absence of randomized controlled trials. It did so when faced with an important clinical practice issue for which persuasive evidence existed. When the panel considered evidence other than randomized controlled trials, it did not restrict itself to articles that otherwise met the inclusion criteria. For example, for recommendations that were not based on meta-analyses, the panel reviewed some articles published after January 1, 1999. This guideline clearly identifies the level or strength of evidence that serves as the basis for each of its recommendations.

Topics Included in the Guideline _____

The panel identified tobacco use as the targeted behavior and tobacco users as the clinical population of interest. Tobacco dependence treatments were evaluated for efficacy as were interventions aimed at modifying both clinician and health care delivery system behavior.

Interventions for the primary prevention of tobacco use were not examined in detail with the exception of interventions directly relevant to clinical practice. Because of the importance and complexity of the primary prevention of tobacco initiation, the panel recommends that primary prevention be addressed in a separate clinical practice guideline. Readers may also refer to the 1994 Surgeon General's Report, *Preventing Tobacco Use Among Young People*.[63] In addition, community-level interventions (e.g., mass media campaigns) that are not usually implemented in primary care practice settings are not addressed. For more information on community-based tobacco use prevention, refer to the *Centers for Disease Control and Prevention Guide to Community Preventive Services* (available in 2000).

This guideline is designed for three main audiences: primary care clinicians; tobacco dependence treatment specialists; and health care administrators, insurers, and purchasers. Additionally, the guideline is designed to be used in a wide variety of clinical practice settings, including private practices, academic health centers, managed care settings and health maintenance organizations, public health department clinics, hospitals, and school or work site clinics.

At the start of the update process, guideline panel members, outside experts, and consortium representatives were consulted to determine those aspects of the original guideline that required updating. These consultations resulted in the following chief recommendations that guided the update efforts: (1) to update any recommendations from the original guideline likely to be affected by new research findings; (2) to provide information and recommendations on health systems changes relevant to tobacco cessation including the cost-effectiveness of tobacco cessation; (3) to summarize the literature and make recommendations regarding special populations; and (4) to address content areas and models of treatment for which little data existed during the development of the original guideline.

Guideline Development Process _____

The original guideline development process was initiated in late 1993. This update was initiated in mid-1998. The methodology was consistent between the two efforts except where specifically identified below (see Figure 1).

Selection of Evidence _____

Published, peer-reviewed, randomized controlled studies were considered to constitute the strongest level of evidence in support of guideline recommendations. This decision was based on the judgment that randomized controlled trials provide the clearest, scientifically sound basis for judging comparative efficacy.

Figure 1. Guideline development process[a]

Literature searches conducted and validated

↓

Abstracts obtained

↓

Abstracts reviewed for inclusion/exclusion criteria by literature reviewers

↓

Full copy of each accepted article read and independently
coded by at least 3 literature reviewers

↓

Evidence tables created by literature reviewers

↓

Initial meta-analyses conducted

↓

Relevant literature and meta-analytic results provided to panel

↓

Panel reviewed evidence, formed tentative
conclusions, identified need for further analyses

↓

Additional literature reviews and meta-analyses conducted by panel staff

↓

Panel reviewed updated evidence

↓

Panel made recommendations based on evidence

↓

Manuscript drafted by panel staff

↓

Manuscript drafts reviewed by panel members

↓

Manuscript draft reviewed by peer reviewers

↓

Manuscript revised and published

[a] These steps were taken in drafting both the original and updated guidelines.

The panel made this decision recognizing the limitations of randomized controlled trials, particularly considerations of generalizability with respect to patient selection and treatment quality.

Literature Review and Inclusion Criteria

Approximately 6,000 articles were reviewed to identify evaluable literature— 3,000 during the original project and another 3,000 during the update. These articles were obtained through searches of electronic databases and reviews of published abstracts and bibliographies. An article was deemed appropriate for meta-analysis if it met the criteria for inclusion established *a priori* by the panel. These criteria were that the article: (a) reported the results of a randomized, placebo/comparison controlled trial of a tobacco-use treatment intervention randomized on the patient level; (b) provided followup results at a timepoint at least 5 months after the quit date; (c) was published in a peer-reviewed journal; (d) was published between January 1, 1975 and January 1, 1999; and (e) was published in English. Additionally, articles screened during the update were screened for relevance to economic or health systems issues. As a result of the original and update literature reviews, more than 180 articles were identified for possible inclusion in a meta-analysis, and more than 500 additional articles were examined by the panel. These articles were used in the consideration and formulation of panel recommendations that were not supported by meta-analyses. The literature search for the update project was validated by comparing the results against a search conducted by the CDC, by a review of the database by the expert panel, and by requesting articles pertaining to special topics from experts in the field.

It is important to note that due to a faithful application of article screening criteria in the updated guideline, some of the studies that were included in the original guideline were not included in the updated analyses. This resulted in an inability to perform certain analyses that had previously been conducted (e.g., analysis of the different types of self-help).

When individual authors published multiple articles meeting the meta-analytic inclusion criteria, the articles were screened to determine whether they contained unique data. Where two articles reported data from the same group of subjects, both articles were used to elicit the complete trial data for the analyses.

Preparation of Evidence Tables _____

Three reviewers independently read and coded each article that met inclusion criteria. The reviewers coded the treatment characteristics that were used in data analyses (see Table 6 in Chapter 6). The same general coding procedure employed during the original guideline process was employed during the update. Where adjustments to the coding process were made, articles from the original process were re-coded to reflect the changed coding (e.g., more refined counseling and behavioral therapy designations were used during the update to capture more specific counseling practices.) The reviewers then met and compared coding. Any discrepancies that could not be resolved were adjudicated by the project director, panel chair, and/or senior scientific consultant. The data were then compiled and used in relevant analyses. As a test of the coding process for the update, inter-rater reliability analyses were conducted on four coded intervention categories: type of format, type of clinician, type of counseling and behavioral therapies, and level of person-to-person contact. Using the proportional overlap method[33] for format, clinician and counseling and behavioral therapies, and the nominal response method[34] for level of person-to-person contact, reliability analyses were conducted on 16 studies that had all been coded by the same three reviewers. Coded data were sampled from the preadjudicated ratings made by the three reviewers who coded the greatest number of articles. Studies and intervention categories were selected after coding, so reviewers were unaware of the data to be analyzed for reliability. Results revealed the following chance-corrected inter-rater reliabilities for each of the tested categories: kappa = .73 for format, kappa = .72 for clinician, kappa = .77 for counseling and behavioral therapies, and kappa = .78 for level of person-to-person contact.

Outcome Data

To meet inclusion criteria for the meta-analyses, a study was required to provide outcome data with followup at least 5 months after the designated quit day. Five months was chosen to balance the needs for (a) a large pool of studies for meta-analyses and (b) the desire to examine only clinically important outcomes (i.e., long-term abstinence). When quit rates were provided for multiple long-term endpoints, efficacy data from the endpoint closest to 6 months were used, so long as they did not exceed 3 years. Virtually all cessation analyses in this guideline were done on these long-term outcome data. (One exception is that the meta-analysis of cessation treatments in pregnant women allowed somewhat shorter followup periods because of the desire for preparturition data.)

Panel staff also coded biochemical confirmation of self-reported abstinence. Previous guideline analyses show that studies with, and without, biochemical confirmation yield similar meta-analysis results. Therefore, meta-analyses presented in the guideline reflect a pooling of these studies. The only exception to this was in the pregnancy analyses. Data suggest that self-reported abstinence rates may be less reliable in pregnant women; therefore, the pregnancy meta-analysis included only abstinence data that were biochemically confirmed.[35-37]

Two types of followup data were included in the analyses to index treatment efficacy. The first and preferred type of data was intent-to-treat data, in which the denominator was the number of patients randomized to treatment and the numerator was the number of abstinent patients contacted at followup. The second type of acceptable data was similar, except that the denominator consisted only of patients who had completed treatment. Other types of followup data were not included in analyses (e.g., studies in which the denominator included only those subjects contacted during followup).

Studies were coded for how the outcome measures were reported, "point prevalence," "continuous," or "unknown." If abstinence data were based on smoking occurrence within a set time period (usually 7 days) prior to a followup assessment, the outcome measure was coded as "point prevalence." "Continuous" was used when a study reported abstinence based on whether study subjects were continuously abstinent from tobacco use since their quit day. "Unknown" was used when it was not possible to discern from the study report whether the authors used a point prevalence or continuous measure for abstinence.

As in the original guideline, a point prevalence outcome measure (1-week point prevalence, when available) rather than continuous abstinence was used as the chief outcome variable. Point prevalence was preferred for several reasons. First, among the 180 randomized controlled trials available for meta-analysis, the majority presented their primary outcome data as point prevalence. Second, continuous abstinence data underestimate the percentage of individuals who are abstinent at particular followup timepoints. They might, therefore, suggest that the likelihood of cessation is lower than in actuality. Finally, most relapse begins early in a quit attempt and persists. A point prevalence measure taken at 5 months would certainly capture the great majority of those relapse events. Therefore, wherever possible, 1-week point prevalence abstinence data were used. If point prevalence data were not available, the preferred alternative was continuous abstinence data. Data of an unknown or unspecified nature were used otherwise.

Meta-Analytic Techniques

The principal analytic technique used in this guideline was meta-analysis. This statistical technique estimates the impact of a treatment or variable across a set of related investigations. The primary meta-analytic model used in this and the original guideline was logistic regression using random effects modeling. The modeling was done at the level of the treatment arm, and study effects were treated as fixed. The panel methodologists chose to employ random effects modeling, assuming that both the subject populations and the treatment elements analyzed would vary from study to study (e.g., "general problemsolving" counseling might be done somewhat differently at two different sites). Random effects modeling is well suited to accommodate such variation among studies.[38] The statistician used the EGRET Logistic Normal Model (Statistics and Epidemiology Research Corporation, *EGRET Reference Manual*, Revision 4, Seattle, 1993). A complete and detailed review of the meta-analytic methods used in the guideline can be found in the *Smoking Cessation Guideline Technical Report No. 18* available from AHRQ as AHCPR Publication No. 97-N004.

The meta-analytic technique assumed randomization of subjects to treatment conditions. Moreover, studies that randomized at another level (e.g., clinician, clinic, etc.) typically did not provide data on nonindependence. Therefore, only studies that randomized at the level of the subject were submitted to meta-analysis. To reduce the likelihood that this selection criterion would bias results, some test analyses were performed that included studies randomized by clinic or clinician. In all cases, these analyses were consistent with the results of studies using subject-based randomization.

The initial step in meta-analysis was the selection of studies that were relevant to the treatment characteristic being evaluated. After relevant studies were identified (e.g., those that contained a self-help intervention if self-help treatments were being evaluated), panel staff reviewed the studies to ensure that they passed screening criteria. Some screening criteria were general (e.g., study presents greater than 5 months followup data), whereas other criteria were specific to the type of treatment characteristic evaluated (e.g., in the analysis of clinicians, screening ensured that differences in type of clinician were not confounded by differences in use of pharmacotherapy). In most cases, there was no attempt to control for the effects of variables that were potentially correlated with an analyzed treatment dimension (e.g., controlling for overall treatment intensity in the analysis of number of types of formats and number of types of clinicians).

The separate arms (treatment or control groups) in each study were then inspected to identify confounders that could compromise interpretation. Seriously confounded arms were excluded from analysis. Relevant characteristics of each arm were then coded to produce meaningful analytic comparisons. Criteria for performing a meta-analysis included: (1) the guideline panel judged the topic to be addressed in the meta-analysis as having substantial clinical significance; (2) at least two studies meeting selection criteria existed on the topic and the studies contained suitable within-study control or comparison conditions; and (3) there was acceptable inter-study homogeneity in the analyzed variable or treatment to permit meaningful inference (e.g., an analyzed treatment was sufficiently similar across various studies so that combining studies was meaningful).

Limitations of Meta-Analytic Techniques. Several factors can compromise the internal validity of meta-analyses. For example, publication biases (particularly the tendency to publish only those studies with positive findings) may result in biased summary statistics. The complement to publication bias is the "file-drawer effect," in which negative or neutral findings are not submitted for publication. In addition, either the magnitude or the significance of the effects of meta-analyses may be influenced by factors such as the frequency with which treatments occurred in the data set, and by the extent to which treatments co-occurred with other treatments. All else being equal, a treatment that occurs infrequently in the data set is less likely to be found significant than a more frequently occurring treatment. Also, when two treatments co-occur frequently in the same groups of subjects, it is difficult to apportion statistically the impact of each. In addition, comparability biases can exist when substantially different groups or treatments are coded as being the same (e.g., when treatments are similar only on a superficial attribute).

Stability of meta-analytic findings was determined with respect to only one population characteristic, that is whether patients sought cessation treatment ("self-selected") or whether treatment was delivered without the patient seeking it ("all-comers," as when cessation treatment occurred as an integral part of health care). Conducting separate meta-analyses in these different subject populations yielded very similar findings across a variety of treatment dimensions (e.g., treatment format, treatment intensity). No other population characteristic (e.g., years smoked, severity of dependence) was explored in meta-analyses.

Interpretation of Meta-Analysis Results. The meta-analyses yielded logistic regression coefficients that were converted to odds ratios. The meaning or interpretation of an odds ratio can be seen most easily by means of an example depicted in a 2 x 2 table. Table 1 contains data showing the relation between maternal smoking and low birth weight in infants. Data are extracted from Hosmer and Lemeshow.[39] The odds of a low birth weight infant if the mother smokes are 30:44, or 0.68 to 1. The odds of a low birth weight infant if the mother does not smoke are 29:86, or 0.34 to 1. The odds ratio is thus $(30/44)/(29/86) = 2.02$ to 1. Therefore, the odds ratio can be seen roughly as the odds of an outcome on one variable, given a certain status on another variable(s). In the case above, the odds of a low birth weight infant is about double for women who smoke compared with those who do not.

Table 1. Relation between maternal smoking and low birth weight in infants

		Maternal smoking		
		Yes	No	
Low birth weight	Yes	30	29	59
	No	44	86	130
		74	115	189

Once odds ratios were obtained from meta-analyses, 95 percent confidence intervals were estimated around the odds ratios. An odds ratio is only an estimate of a relation between variables. The 95 percent confidence interval presents an estimate of the accuracy of the particular odds ratio obtained. If the 95 percent confidence interval for a given odds ratio does not include "1," then the odds ratio represents a statistically significant effect at the .05 level. The confidence intervals will generally not be perfectly symmetrical around an odds ratio because of the distributional properties of the odds ratio. Comparisons of the relative sizes of odds ratios is meaningful only for those odds ratios yielded by the same meta-analysis (listed in the same data table).

After computing the odds ratios and their confidence intervals, the odds ratios were converted to abstinence percentages and their 95 percent confidence intervals (based on reference category abstinence rates). Abstinence percentages indicate the estimated long-term abstinence rate achieved under the tested treatment or treatment characteristic. The abstinence percentage results are approximate estimates derived from the odds ratio data.[40] Therefore, they essentially duplicate the odds ratio results but are presented because their meaning may be clearer for some readers. Because the placebo/control abstinence percentage for a particular analysis is calculated exclusively from the studies included within that meta-analysis, these abstinence percentages vary across the different analyses.

How To Read the Data Tables

Table 2 depicts a table of results from one of the meta-analyses reported in this guideline. This table presents results from the analysis of the effects of different treatment formats on outcome (see Formats of Psychosocial Treatments in Chapter 6B). In this table, the comparison condition, or "reference group," for determining the impact of different treatment options, was smokers who had no contact with a provider. The "Estimated odds ratio" column reveals that treatment groups receiving self-help treatment had an odds ratio of 1.2. The odds ratio indicates a significant effect, because the lower boundary of the confidence interval did not include "1." Proactive phone counseling had an odds ratio of 1.2, and group counseling had an odds ratio of 1.3. Both of these are statistically significant because the lower bounds of their confidence intervals do

Table 2. Meta-analysis: Efficacy of and estimated abstinence rates for various types of format (n = 58 studies)

Format	Number of arms	Estimated odds ratio (95% C.I.)	Estimated abstinence rate (95% C.I.)
No format	20	1.0	10.8
Self-help	93	1.2 (1.02, 1.3)	12.3 (10.9, 13.6)
Proactive telephone counseling	26	1.2 (1.1, 1.4)	13.1 (11.4, 14.8)
Group counseling	52	1.3 (1.1, 1.6)	13.9 (11.6, 16.1)
Individual counseling	67	1.7 (1.4, 2.0)	16.8 (14.7, 19.1)

not include "1". Individual counseling had the largest odds ratio of 1.7. This odds ratio means that when a smoker receives individual counseling, he or she is more than one and one-half times more likely to remain abstinent than if he or she had received no counseling.

The column labeled "Estimated abstinence rate" shows the abstinence percentages for the various treatment formats. For instance, the reference group conditions (no contact) in the analyzed data set were associated with an abstinence rate of 10.8 percent. Consistent with the odds ratio data reviewed above, self-help treatments produced modest increases in abstinence rates (12.3 percent), proactive phone counseling and group counseling produced somewhat larger increases in abstinence rates (13.1 percent and 13.9 percent respectively), and individual counseling produced the largest increase (16.8 percent).

The total number of studies included in each meta-analysis is provided within the title of the corresponding table. A list of published articles used in each meta-analysis is available from AHRQ via the AHRQ Web site at www.ahrq.gov.

The column labeled "Number of arms" lists the number of treatment conditions or groups across all analyzed studies that contributed data to the various treatment format categories (e.g., self-help treatment was provided in 93 treatment arms). Therefore, this column depicts the number of treatment conditions or groups relevant to each analyzed category. Frequently, the number of treatment groups or arms exceeds the number of studies included in a meta-analysis.

The outcome data in the tables include studies with "all-comers" (individuals who did not seek a treatment intervention) and "self-selected" populations, studies using point-prevalence and continuous abstinence endpoints, and studies with and without biochemical confirmation, except where otherwise described. Some meta-analyses (such as those evaluating pharmacotherapies) included predominantly studies with "self-selected" populations. In addition, in pharmacotherapy studies both experimental and control subjects typically received substantial counseling.

Both of these factors tend to produce higher abstinence rates in reference or placebo subjects than are typically observed among self-quitters.

Strength of Evidence

Every recommendation made by the panel bears a strength-of-evidence rating that indicates the quality and quantity of empirical support for the recommendation. Each recommendation and its strength of evidence reflect consensus of the guideline panel. The three strength of evidence ratings are described below:

A   Multiple well-designed randomized clinical trials, directly relevant to the recommendation, yielded a consistent pattern of findings.

B   Some evidence from randomized clinical trials supported the recommendation, but the scientific support was not optimal. For instance, few randomized trials existed, the trials that did exist were somewhat inconsistent, or the trials were not directly relevant to the recommendation.

C   Reserved for important clinical situations where the panel achieved consensus on the recommendation in the absence of relevant randomized controlled trials.

The availability of randomized clinical trials was not considered in economic recommendations. The existence of such trials was thought to be a less germane criterion for evaluating economic studies. In such cases, the strength of evidence is based primarily on the consistency of findings among different studies. Finally, the panel declined to make recommendations when there was no relevant evidence or the evidence was too weak or inconsistent to support a recommendation.

Caveats Regarding Recommendations

The reader should note some caveats regarding guideline recommendations. First, an absence of studies should not be confused with proven lack of efficacy. In certain situations, there was little direct evidence regarding the efficacy of some treatments, and in these cases the panel usually rendered no opinion. Second, even when there were enough studies to perform a meta-analysis, a nonsignificant result does not prove inefficacy. Rather, nonsignificance merely indicates that efficacy was not demonstrated given the data available.

The emphasis of this guideline was to identify efficacious interventions, not to rank-order interventions in terms of efficacy. The panel chose not to emphasize comparisons among efficacious interventions for several reasons. First, the most important goal of the analytic process was to identify all efficacious interventions. Second, selection or use of particular intervention techniques or strategies is usually a function of practical factors: patient preference, time available, training of the clinician, cost, and so on. The panel believed clinicians should choose the most appropriate intervention from among the efficacious interventions, given existing circumstances. An excessive emphasis on relative efficacy might discourage clinicians from using interventions that have a small, but reliable, impact on smoking cessation. Finally, data were often inadequate or unavailable to make adequate statistical comparisons of different types of interventions. For example, there were insufficient studies testing head-to-head comparisons of the different pharmacotherapies to allow a rank-ordering of the different pharmacotherapies.

Despite a lack of emphasis on the rank-ordering of interventions, some interventions were so superior to control or no-treatment conditions that the panel clearly identified them as superior to another intervention. For instance, although minimal person-to-person contact can increase smoking abstinence rates over no-treatment conditions, there is little doubt that longer person-to-person interventions have greater impact.

External Review of the Guideline

The panel and AHRQ invited 155 outside reviewers to review the draft of the 1996 guideline. In addition, AHRQ placed a notice in the *Federal Register* inviting individuals to review and comment on this original draft guideline. A total of 71 reviewers provided comments. Panel and consortium members invited 175 outside reviewers to review the updated guideline. A total of 70 provided comments. Peer reviewers included clinicians, health care administrators, social workers, counselors, health educators, researchers, consumers, key personnel at selected Federal agencies, and others. Reviewers were asked to evaluate the guideline based on five criteria: validity, reliability, clarity, clinical applicability, and utility. Comments of the peer reviewers were incorporated into the guideline when appropriate.

Guideline Products

Accompanying the original guideline were four products intended to aid in the dissemination and translation of the guideline's evidence-based recommendations. These products were intended to address consumers as well as the three target audiences: primary care clinicians, specialists, health care administrators, insurers, and purchasers. These products were: (1) *You Can Quit Smoking. Consumer Guide*; (2) *Helping Smokers Quit. A Guide for Primary Care Clinicians*; (3) *Smoking Cessation: Information for Specialists. Quick Reference Guide*; and (4) *Smoking Cessation, A Systems Approach: A Guide for Health Care Administrators, Insurers, Managed Care Organizations, and Purchasers*. Similar products will disseminate the recommendations of the updated guideline.

Organization of the Guideline Update

This updated guideline is divided into eight chapters that reflect the major components of tobacco dependence treatment (see Figure 2 for treatment model):

Chapter 1, Overview and Methods, provides an overview and rationale for the updated guideline, as well as a detailed description of the methodology used to review the scientific literature and develop the original and updated guidelines.

Chapter 2, Assessment of Tobacco Use, establishes the importance of determining the tobacco use status of every patient at every visit.

Chapter 3, Brief Clinical Interventions, is intended to provide clinicians with guidance as they use brief interventions to treat tobacco users willing to quit, tobacco users unwilling to make a quit attempt at this time, and tobacco users who have recently quit.

A. For the Patient Willing To Quit, provides brief clinical approaches to assist patients in quit attempts.

B. For the Patient Unwilling To Quit, provides brief clinical approaches designed to motivate the patient to make a quit attempt at this time.

C. For the Patient Who Has Recently Quit, provides clinicians with brief strategies designed to reinforce an ex-tobacco user's commitment to stay tobacco-free.

Chapter 4, Intensive Clinical Interventions, provides clinicians with more intensive strategies to treat tobacco users.

Chapter 5, Systems Interventions: Relevance to Health Care Administrators, Insurers, and Purchasers, is directed at health care administrators, insurers, purchasers, and other decisionmakers who can affect health care systems. This chapter provides these decisionmakers with strategies to modify health care systems to improve the delivery of tobacco treatment services.

Chapter 6, Evidence, presents the evidentiary basis for the updated guideline recommendations.

A. Screening and Assessment, provides recommendations and analysis results regarding screening for tobacco use and specialized assessment.

B. Treatment Structure and Intensity, provides recommendations and analysis results regarding advice, intensity of clinical interventions, and type of clinician, format, and followup procedures.

C. Treatment Elements, provides recommendations and analysis results regarding types of counseling and behavioral therapies and pharmaco-therapy.

Chapter 7, Special Populations, provides information on specific populations such as women, pregnant tobacco users, racial and ethnic minorities, hospitalized patients, older adults, tobacco users with other chemical dependencies, and children and adolescents.

Chapter 8, Special Topics, provides specific information on topics not otherwise addressed in the updated guideline such as weight gain associated with tobacco cessation, noncigarette tobacco products, clinician training, and reimbursement for tobacco cessation treatment.

Figure 2. Model for treatment of tobacco use and dependence

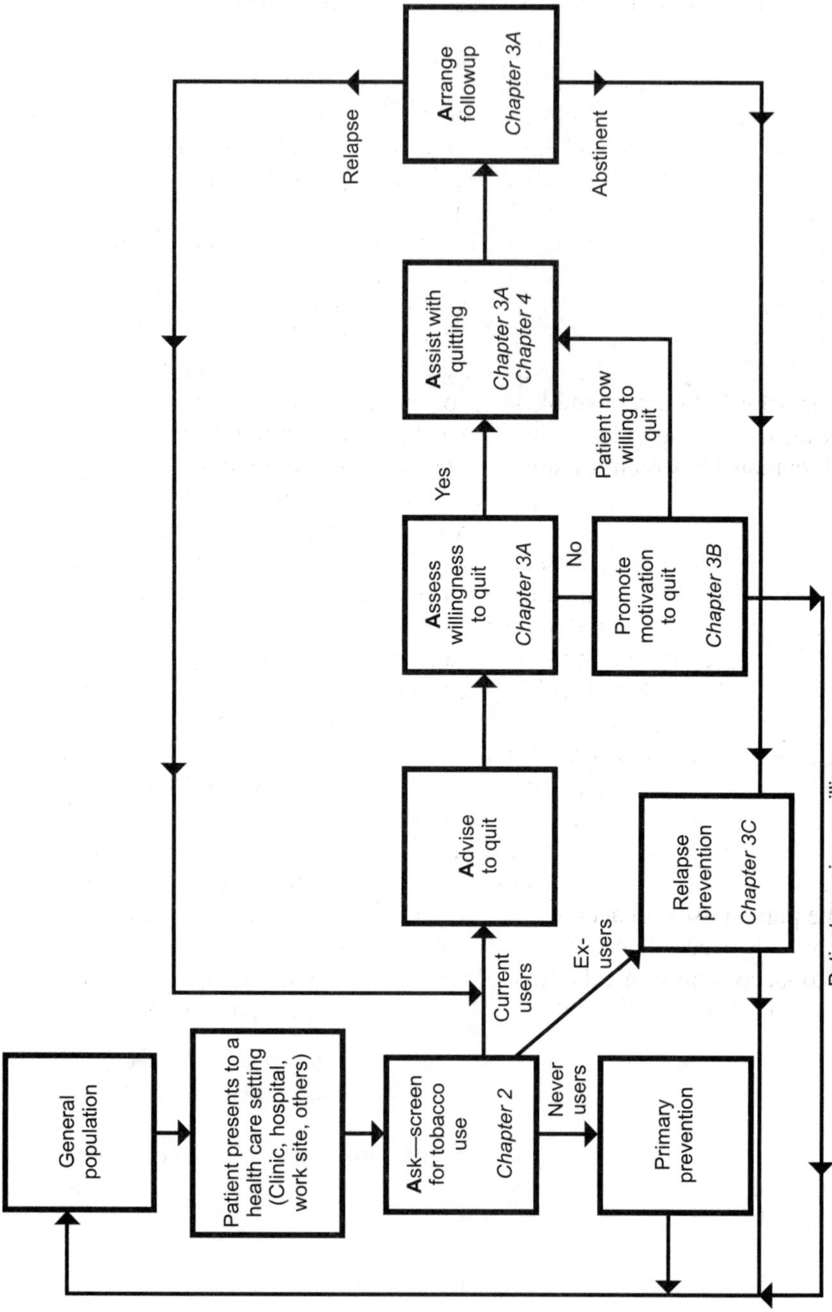

2 Assessment of Tobacco Use

At least 70 percent of smokers see a physician each year, and more than 50 percent see a dentist.[41-43] Other smokers see physician assistants, nurse practitioners, nurses, physical and occupational therapists, pharmacists, and other clinicians. Therefore, all clinicians, particularly physicians and dentists, are uniquely poised to intervene with patients who use tobacco. Moreover, 70 percent of smokers report wanting to quit.[3] Finally, smokers cite a physician's advice to quit as an important motivator for attempting to stop smoking.[44-46] These data suggest that most smokers are interested in quitting, clinicians are frequently in contact with smokers, and clinicians have high credibility with smokers.

Unfortunately, clinicians are not capitalizing on this unique opportunity. More than one-third of current smokers report never having been asked about their smoking status or urged to quit.[11,47] Moreover, a population-based survey found that less than 15 percent of smokers who saw a physician in the past year were offered assistance, and only 3 percent had a followup appointment to address tobacco use.[48] Fewer still have received specific advice on how to quit smoking successfully. This guideline clearly identifies empirically validated tobacco treatment strategies to spur clinicians, tobacco treatment specialists, and administrators to intervene effectively with patients who use tobacco.

The first step in treating tobacco use and dependence is to identify tobacco users. As the data analysis in Chapter 6 shows, the identification of smokers itself increases rates of clinician intervention. Effective identification of tobacco use status not only opens the door for successful interventions (e.g., physician advice), but also it guides clinicians to identify appropriate interventions based on patients' tobacco use status and willingness to quit.

Screening for current or past tobacco use will result in four possible responses: (1) the patient uses tobacco and is now willing to make a quit attempt; (2) the patient uses tobacco but is not now willing to make a quit attempt; (3) the patient once used tobacco but has since quit; and (4) the patient never regularly used tobacco. This clinical practice guideline is organized to provide the clinician with simple, but effective interventions for all of these patients (see Figure 3).

Figure 3. Algorithm for treating tobacco use

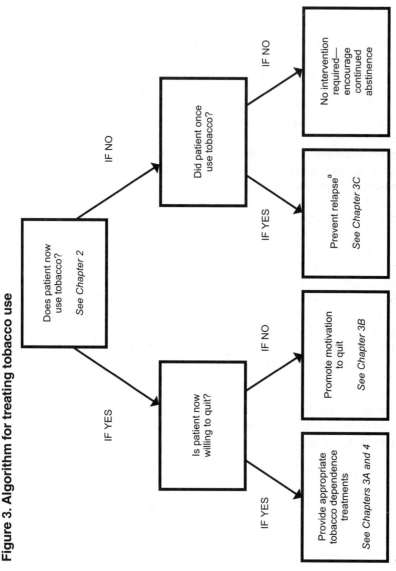

a Relapse prevention interventions are not necessary in the case of the adult who has not used tobacco for many years.

3 Brief Clinical Interventions

Background

This section of the guideline presents specific strategies to guide clinicians providing brief interventions. These brief interventions can be provided by any clinician but are most relevant to primary care clinicians (physicians, nurses, dentists, hygienists, respiratory therapists, pharmacists, etc.) who see a wide variety of patients, and who are bound by time constraints. These strategies are based on the evidence described in Chapters 6, 7, and 8, as well as on panel opinion. Guideline analysis suggests that a wide variety of clinicians can implement these brief strategies effectively. The goals of these strategies are clear: to change clinical culture and practice patterns to ensure that every patient who uses tobacco is identified and offered treatment. The strategies underscore a central theme: it is essential to provide at least a brief intervention to all tobacco users at each clinical visit. Several observations are relevant to this theme. First, institutional changes in clinical practice are necessary to ensure that all patients who use tobacco are identified for intervention (see Chapter 5, Systems Interventions: Relevance to Health Care Administrators, Insurers, and Purchasers). Second, the compelling time limits on primary care physicians in the United States today[49] (median visit = 12 to 16 minutes)[50] often require brief interventions, although more intensive interventions would produce greater success. Third, although many smokers are reluctant to seek intensive cessation programs,[51] they nevertheless can receive a brief intervention every time they visit a clinician.[22]

This Chapter is divided into three sections to guide brief clinician interventions with three types of patients: (A) current tobacco users now willing to make a quit attempt; (B) current tobacco users unwilling at this time to make a quit attempt; and (C) former tobacco users who have recently quit. Adults who have never used tobacco or who have been abstinent for an extended period do not require intervention. The clinician may congratulate them on their status and encourage them to maintain their tobacco-free lifestyle.

A. For the Patient Willing To Quit

Given that so many tobacco users visit a primary care clinician each year, it is important that these clinicians be prepared to intervene with tobacco users who are willing to quit. The five major steps (the "5 A's") to intervention in the primary care setting are listed in Table 3. It is important for the clinician to *ask* the patient if he or she uses tobacco (Brief Strategy A1), *advise* him or her to quit (Brief Strategy A2), *assess* willingness to make a quit attempt (Brief Strategy A3), *assist* him or her in making a quit attempt (Brief Strategy A4), and *arrange* for followup contacts to prevent relapse (Brief Strategy A5). The strategies are designed to be brief, requiring 3 minutes or less of direct clinician time. Office systems that institutionalize tobacco use assessment and intervention will greatly

Table 3. The "5 A's" for brief intervention

Ask about tobacco use.	Identify and document tobacco use status for every patient at every visit. (Brief Strategy A1)
Advise to quit.	In a clear, strong and personalized manner urge every tobacco user to quit. (Brief Strategy A2)
Assess willingness to make a quit attempt.	Is the tobacco user willing to make a quit attempt at this time? (Brief Strategy A3)
Assist in quit attempt.	For the patient willing to make a quit attempt, use counseling and pharmacotherapy to help him or her quit. (Brief Strategy A4)
Arrange followup.	Schedule followup contact, preferably within the first week after the quit date. (Brief Strategy A5)

foster the adoption of these strategies (see Chapter 5). Finally, these strategies are consistent with those produced by the NCI[13,52] and the American Medical Association,[27] as well as others.[26,53,54]

In addition to counseling, all smokers making a quit attempt should receive pharmacotherapy, except in the presence of special circumstances. See Table 4 for guidelines for prescribing pharmacotherapy for smoking cessation.

Table 4. Clinical guidelines for prescribing pharmacotherapy for smoking cessation

Who should receive pharmacotherapy for smoking cessation?	All smokers trying to quit, except in the presence of special circumstances. Special consideration should be given before using pharmacotherapy with selected populations: those with medical contraindications, those smoking fewer than 10 cigarettes/day, pregnant/breastfeeding women, and adolescent smokers.
What are the first-line pharmacotherapies recommended in this guideline?	All five of the FDA-approved pharmacotherapies for smoking cessation are recommended, including bupropion SR, nicotine gum, nicotine inhaler, nicotine nasal spray, and the nicotine patch.
What factors should a clinician consider when choosing among the five first-line pharmacotherapies?	Because of the lack of sufficient data to rank-order these five medications, choice of a specific first-line pharmacotherapy must be guided by factors such as clinician familiarity with the medications, contraindications for selected patients, patient preference, previous patient experience with a specific pharmacotherapy (positive or negative), and patient characteristics (e.g., history of depression, concerns about weight gain).

Table 4. Clinical guidelines for prescribing pharmacotherapy for smoking cessation (continued)

Are pharmaco-therapeutic treatments appropriate for lighter smokers (e.g., 10-15 cigarettes/day)?	If pharmacotherapy is used with lighter smokers, clinicians should consider reducing the dose of first-line NRT pharmacotherapies. No adjustments are necessary when using bupropion SR.
What second-line pharmacotherapies are recommended in this guideline?	Clonidine and nortriptyline.
When should second-line agents be used for treating tobacco dependence?	Consider prescribing second-line agents for patients unable to use first-line medications because of contraindications or for patients for whom first-line medications are not helpful. Monitor patients for the known side effects of second-line agents.
Which pharmaco-therapies should be considered with patients particularly concerned about weight gain?	Bupropion SR and nicotine replacement therapies, in particular nicotine gum, have been shown to delay, but not prevent, weight gain.
Are there pharmaco-therapies that should be especially considered in patients with a history of depression?	Bupropion SR and nortriptyline appear to be effective with this population.
Should nicotine replacement therapies be avoided in patients with a history of cardiovascular disease?	No. The nicotine patch in particular is safe and has been shown not to cause adverse cardiovascular effects.
May tobacco dependence pharmacotherapies be used long-term (e.g., 6 months or more)?	Yes. This approach may be helpful with smokers who report persistent withdrawal symptoms during the course of pharmacotherapy or who desire long-term therapy. A minority of individuals who successfully quit smoking use ad libitum NRT medications (gum, nasal spray, inhaler) long-term. The use of these medications long-term does not present a known health risk. Additionally, the FDA has approved the use of bupropion SR for a long-term maintenance indication.
May pharmaco-therapies ever be combined?	Yes. There is evidence that combining the nicotine patch with either nicotine gum or nicotine nasal spray increases long-term abstinence rates over those produced by a single form of NRT.

Brief Strategies: Helping the Patient Willing To Quit _____

Brief Strategy A1. Ask—systematically identify all tobacco users at every visit

Action	Strategies for implementation
Implement an office-wide system that ensures that, for EVERY patient at EVERY clinic visit, tobacco-use status is queried and documented.[a]	Expand the vital signs to include tobacco use or use an alternative universal identification system.[b] **VITAL SIGNS** Blood Pressure: _____ Pulse: _____ Weight: _____ Temperature: _____ Respiratory Rate: _____ Tobacco Use: Current Former Never (circle one) [b] Alternatives to expanding the vital signs are to place tobacco-use status stickers on all patient charts or to indicate tobacco use status using electronic medical records or computer reminder systems.

[a] Repeated assessment is *not* necessary in the case of the adult who has never used tobacco or has not used tobacco for many years, and for whom this information is clearly documented in the medical record.

Brief Strategy A2. Advise—strongly urge all tobacco users to quit

Action	Strategies for implementation
In a *clear, strong,* and *personalized* manner, urge every tobacco user to quit.	Advice should be: ■ *Clear*—"I think it is important for you to quit smoking now and I can help you." "Cutting down while you are ill is not enough." ■ *Strong*—"As your clinician, I need you to know that quitting smoking is the most important thing you can do to protect your health now and in the future. The clinic staff and I will help you." ■ *Personalized*—Tie tobacco use to current health/illness, and/or its social and economic costs, motivation level/readiness to quit, and/or the impact of tobacco use on children and others in the household.

Brief Strategy A3. Assess—determine willingness to make a quit attempt

Action	Strategies for implementation
Ask every tobacco user if he or she is willing to make a quit attempt at this time (e.g., within the next 30 days).	Assess patient's willingness to quit: ■ If the patient is willing to make a quit attempt at this time, provide assistance (see Chapter 3A, Brief Strategy A4). ■ If the patient will participate in an intensive treatment, deliver such a treatment or refer to an intensive intervention (see Chapter 4). ■ If the patient clearly states he or she is unwilling to make a quit attempt at this time, provide a motivational intervention (see Chapter 3B). ■ If the patient is a member of a special population (e.g., adolescent, pregnant smoker, racial/ethnic minority), consider providing additional information (see Chapter 7).

Brief Strategy A4. Assist—aid the patient in quitting

Action	Strategies for implementation
Help the patient with a quit plan.	*A patient's preparations for quitting:* ■ *Set a quit date*—ideally, the quit date should be within 2 weeks. ■ *Tell* family, friends, and coworkers about quitting and request understanding and support. ■ *Anticipate* challenges to planned quit attempt, particularly during the critical first few weeks. These include nicotine withdrawal symptoms. ■ *Remove* tobacco products from your environment. Prior to quitting, avoid smoking in places where you spend a lot of time (e.g., work, home, car).

Brief Strategy A4. Assist—aid the patient in quitting (continued)

Provide practical counseling (problemsolving/ skills training).	*Abstinence*—Total abstinence is essential. "Not even a single puff after the quit date."
	Past quit experience—Identify what helped and what hurt in previous quit attempts.
	Anticipate triggers or challenges in upcoming attempt— Discuss challenges/triggers and how patient will successfully overcome them.
	Alcohol—Since alcohol can cause relapse, the patient should consider limiting/abstaining from alcohol while quitting.
	Other smokers in the household—Quitting is more difficult when there is another smoker in the household. Patients should encourage housemates to quit with them or not smoke in their presence.
Provide intra-treatment social support.	Provide a supportive clinical environment while encouraging the patient in his or her quit attempt. "My office staff and I are available to assist you." (See Table 22)
Help patient obtain extra-treatment social support.	Help patient develop social support for his or her quit attempt in his or her environments outside of treatment. "Ask your spouse/partner, friends, and coworkers to support you in your quit attempt." (See Table 23)
Recommend the use of approved pharmacotherapy, except in special circumstances.	Recommend the use of pharmacotherapies found to be effective in this guideline (see Table 4 for clinical guidelines and Tables 33-39 for specific instructions and precautions). Explain how these medications increase smoking cessation success and reduce withdrawal symptoms. The first-line pharmacotherapy medications include: bupropion SR, nicotine gum, nicotine inhaler, nicotine nasal spray, and nicotine patch.
Provide supplementary materials.	*Sources*—Federal agencies, nonprofit agencies, or local/state health departments (see Appendix A for Web site addresses).
	Type—Culturally/racially/educationally/age appropriate for the patient.
	Location—Readily available at every clinician's workstation.

Brief Strategy A5. Arrange—schedule followup contact

Action	Strategies for implementation
Schedule followup contact, either in person or via telephone.	*Timing*—Followup contact should occur soon after the quit date, preferably during the first week. A second followup contact is recommended within the first month. Schedule further followup contacts as indicated.
	Actions during followup contact—Congratulate success. If tobacco use has occurred, review circumstances and elicit recommitment to total abstinence. Remind patient that a lapse can be used as a learning experience. Identify problems already encountered and anticipate challenges in the immediate future. Assess pharmacotherapy use and problems. Consider use or referral to more intensive treatment (see Chapter 4).

B. For the Patient Unwilling To Quit

Promoting the Motivation To Quit

All patients entering a health care setting should have their tobacco use status assessed routinely. Clinicians should advise all tobacco users to quit and then assess a patient's willingness to make a quit attempt. For patients not ready to make a quit attempt at this time, clinicians should use a brief intervention designed to promote the motivation to quit.

Patients unwilling to make a quit attempt during a visit may lack information about the harmful effects of tobacco, may lack the required financial resources, may have fears or concerns about quitting, or may be demoralized because of previous relapse.[55] Such patients may respond to a motivational intervention that provides the clinician an opportunity to educate, reassure, and motivate such as the motivational intervention built around the "5 R's": *relevance, risks, rewards, roadblocks,* and *repetition.* Clinical components of the "5 R's" are shown in Brief Strategy B below. Motivational interventions are most likely to be successful when the clinician is *empathic, promotes patient autonomy* (e.g., choice among options), *avoids arguments,* and *supports the patient's self-efficacy* (e.g., by identifying previous successes in behavior change efforts).[56-58]

Brief Strategy B. Enhancing motivation to quit tobacco—the "5 R's"

Relevance	Encourage the patient to indicate why quitting is personally relevant, being as specific as possible. Motivational information has the greatest impact if it is relevant to a patient's disease status or risk, family or social situation (e.g., having children in the home), health concerns, age, gender, and other important patient characteristics (e.g., prior quitting experience, personal barriers to cessation).
Risks	The clinician should ask the patient to identify potential negative consequences of tobacco use. The clinician may suggest and highlight those that seem most relevant to the patient. The clinician should emphasize that smoking low-tar/low-nicotine cigarettes or use of other forms of tobacco (e.g., smokeless tobacco, cigars, and pipes) will not eliminate these risks. Examples of risks are: ■ *Acute risks:* Shortness of breath, exacerbation of asthma, harm to pregnancy, impotence, infertility, increased serum carbon monoxide. ■ *Long-term risks:* Heart attacks and strokes, lung and other cancers (larynx, oral cavity, pharynx, esophagus, pancreas, bladder, cervix), chronic obstructive pulmonary diseases (chronic bronchitis and emphysema), long-term disability and need for extended care. ■ *Environmental risks:* Increased risk of lung cancer and heart disease in spouses; higher rates of smoking by children of tobacco users; increased risk for low birth weight, SIDS, asthma, middle ear disease, and respiratory infections in children of smokers.
Rewards	The clinician should ask the patient to identify potential benefits of stopping tobacco use. The clinician may suggest and highlight those that seem most relevant to the patient. Examples of rewards follow: ■ Improved health. ■ Food will taste better. ■ Improved sense of smell. ■ Save money. ■ Feel better about yourself. ■ Home, car, clothing, breath will smell better. ■ Can stop worrying about quitting. ■ Set a good example for children.

**Brief Strategy B. Enhancing motivation to quit tobacco—
the "5 R's" (continued)**

	■ Have healthier babies and children.
	■ Not worry about exposing others to smoke.
	■ Feel better physically.
	■ Perform better in physical activities.
	■ Reduced wrinkling/aging of skin.
Roadblocks	The clinician should ask the patient to identify barriers or impediments to quitting and note elements of treatment (problemsolving, pharmacotherapy) that could address barriers. Typical barriers might include: ■ Withdrawal symptoms. ■ Fear of failure. ■ Weight gain. ■ Lack of support. ■ Depression. ■ Enjoyment of tobacco.
Repetition	The motivational intervention should be repeated every time an unmotivated patient visits the clinic setting. Tobacco users who have failed in previous quit attempts should be told that most people make repeated quit attempts before they are successful.

C. For the Patient Who Has Recently Quit

Preventing Relapse_____

Because of the chronic relapsing nature of tobacco dependence, clinicians should provide brief effective relapse prevention treatment. When clinicians encounter a patient who has quit tobacco use recently, they should reinforce the patient's decision to quit, review the benefits of quitting, and assist the patient in resolving any residual problems arising from quitting. Although most relapse occurs early in the quitting process,[59,60] some relapse occurs months or even years after the quit date.[31,61] Therefore, clinicians should engage in relapse prevention interventions even with former tobacco users who no longer consider themselves actively engaged in the quitting process.

Relapse prevention interventions are especially important soon after quitting and can be delivered by means of either scheduled clinic visits, telephone calls, or any time the clinician encounters an ex-tobacco user. A systematic, institutionalized mechanism to identify recent quitters and contact them is essential to deliver relapse prevention messages effectively.

Relapse prevention interventions can be divided into two categories: minimal practice and prescriptive interventions.

Minimal Practice Interventions. Minimal practice relapse prevention interventions should be part of every encounter with a patient who has quit recently (Brief Strategy C1). These interventions are appropriate for most recent quitters and can be addressed briefly during a coincident clinic visit or a scheduled followup visit. Because most relapse occurs within the first 3 months after quitting, relapse prevention is especially appropriate during this period.[62,63] In addition, strategies designed to reduce relapse should be included in the initial preparation for a quit attempt (see Chapter 3A, Brief Strategy A4. Assist: Aid the patient in quitting, and Chapter 3B, Brief Strategy B. Enhancing motivation to quit tobacco – the "5 R's"). Finally, encourage patients to report difficulties promptly (e.g., lapses, depression, medication side-effects) while continuing efforts to quit.

Prescriptive Interventions. Prescriptive relapse prevention components are individualized based on information obtained about problems the patient has encountered in maintaining abstinence (Brief Strategy C2). These more intensive relapse prevention interventions may be delivered during a dedicated followup contact (in-person or by telephone) or through a specialized clinic or program.

Brief Strategies: Preventing Relapse to Tobacco Use _____

Brief Strategy C1. Components of minimal practice relapse prevention

These interventions should be part of every encounter with a patient who has quit recently:

Every ex-tobacco user undergoing relapse prevention should receive congratulations on any success and strong encouragement to remain abstinent.

When encountering a recent quitter, use open-ended questions designed to initiate patient problemsolving (e.g., How has stopping tobacco use helped you?). The clinician should encourage the patients' *active* discussion of the topics below:

- The benefits, including potential health benefits, the patient may derive from cessation.

- Any success the patient has had in quitting (duration of abstinence, reduction in withdrawal, etc.).

- The problems encountered or anticipated threats to maintaining abstinence (e.g., depression, weight gain, alcohol, other tobacco users in the household).

Brief Strategy C2. Components of prescriptive relapse prevention

During prescriptive relapse prevention, a patient might identify a problem that threatens his or her abstinence. Specific problems likely to be reported by patients and potential responses follow:

Problems	Responses
Lack of support for cessation	■ Schedule followup visits or telephone calls with the patient. ■ Help the patient identify sources of support within his or her environment. ■ Refer the patient to an appropriate organization that offers cessation counseling or support.
Negative mood or depression	■ If significant, provide counseling, prescribe appropriate medications, or refer the patient to a specialist.
Strong or prolonged withdrawal symptoms	■ If the patient reports prolonged craving or other withdrawal symptoms, consider extending the use of an approved pharmacotherapy or adding/combining pharmacologic medications to reduce strong withdrawal symptoms.
Weight gain	■ Recommend starting or increasing physical activity; discourage strict dieting. ■ Reassure the patient that some weight gain after quitting is common and appears to be self-limiting. ■ Emphasize the importance of a healthy diet. ■ Maintain the patient on pharmacotherapy known to delay weight gain (e.g., bupropion SR, NRTs, particularly nicotine gum). ■ Refer the patient to a specialist or program.
Flagging motivation/ feeling deprived	■ Reassure the patient that these feelings are common. ■ Recommend rewarding activities. ■ Probe to ensure that the patient is not engaged in periodic tobacco use. ■ Emphasize that beginning to smoke (even a puff) will increase urges and make quitting more difficult.

4 Intensive Clinical Interventions

Background

Intensive tobacco dependence treatment can be provided by any suitably trained clinician who has the resources available to give intensive interventions. Based on the evidence in Chapter 6, it has been shown that more intensive tobacco dependence treatment is more effective than brief treatment. Also, it should be noted that intensive interventions are appropriate for any tobacco user willing to participate in them. There is no evidence that the efficacy or cost-effectiveness of intensive interventions is limited to a subpopulation of tobacco users (e.g., heavily dependent smokers).[64]

In many cases, intensive tobacco dependence interventions are provided by clinicians who specialize in the treatment of tobacco dependence. Such specialists are not defined by their professional affiliation or by the field in which they trained. Rather, specialists view tobacco dependence treatment as a primary professional role. Specialists possess the skills, knowledge, and training to provide efficacious interventions across a range of intensities, and are often affiliated with programs offering intensive treatment interventions or services (programs with staff dedicated to tobacco interventions, where treatment involves multiple counseling sessions, and so on). In addition to offering intensive treatments, specialists often conduct research on tobacco dependence and its treatment.

As noted above, there is substantial evidence that intensive interventions produce higher success rates than do less intensive interventions (as indicated by several findings of this guideline). In addition, the tobacco dependence interventions offered by specialists represent an important treatment resource for patients who do not receive tobacco dependence treatment from their primary care clinician.

Although the specialist contributes greatly to tobacco treatment efforts, constraints limit the impact of the specialist's service delivery activities. For example, only a minority of smokers participate in the intensive programs typically offered by specialists.[51,65] This suggests that, in the future, the specialist may contribute to tobacco treatment efforts through activities such as the following:

- Serving as a resource to nonspecialists who offer tobacco dependence services as part of general health care delivery. This might include training nonspecialists in counseling strategies, providing consultation on difficult cases and for inpatients, and providing specialized assessment services.

- Developing and evaluating changes in office/clinic procedures that increase the rates at which tobacco users are identified and treated.

- Conducting evaluation research to determine the effectiveness of ongoing tobacco dependence treatment activities in relevant institutional settings.

- Developing and evaluating innovative treatment strategies that may increase the effectiveness and utilization of tobacco dependence treatments.

Strategies for Intensive Tobacco Dependence Intervention

Table 5 highlights guideline findings based on analyses found in Chapter 6, as well as on panel opinion, that seem particularly relevant to the implementation of intensive treatment programs. The findings from Table 5 lead to the development of an intensive treatment strategy (see Intensive Strategy. Components of an intensive intervention). Of course, implementation of this strategy depends on factors such as resource availability and time constraints.

Table 5. Findings relevant to intensive interventions

■ There is a strong dose-response relation between counseling intensity and cessation success. In general, the more intense the treatment intervention, the greater the rate of smoking cessation. Treatments may be made more intense by increasing (a) the length of individual treatment sessions and (b) the number of treatment sessions.
■ Many different types of providers (physicians, nurses, dentists, psychologists, pharmacists, etc.) are effective in increasing rates of tobacco cessation, and involving multiple types of providers may enhance abstinence rates.
■ Proactive telephone calls and individual and group counseling are effective tobacco cessation formats.
■ Particular types of counseling and behavioral therapies are especially effective. Practical counseling (problemsolving/skills-training approaches), and the provision of intra-treatment and extra-treatment social support are associated with significant increases in abstinence rates, as are aversive smoking techniques (e.g., rapid smoking).
■ Pharmacotherapies such as bupropion SR or nicotine replacement therapies consistently increase abstinence rates. Therefore, their use should be encouraged for all quitters, but special consideration is required with some populations (e.g., pregnant smokers, adolescents).
■ Tobacco dependence treatments are effective across diverse populations (e.g., populations varying on gender, age, and ethnicity).

Intensive Strategy. Components of an intensive intervention

Assessment	Assessments should ensure that tobacco users are willing to make a quit attempt using an intensive treatment program. Other assessments can provide information useful in counseling (e.g., stress level, presence of comorbidity; see Chapter 6A, Specialized Assessment).
Program clinicians	Multiple types of clinicians are effective and should be used. One counseling strategy would be to have a medical/health care clinician deliver messages about health risks and benefits and deliver pharmacotherapy, and nonmedical clinicians deliver additional psychosocial or behavioral interventions.
Program intensity	Because of evidence of a strong dose-response relation, the intensity of the program should be: *Session length*—longer than 10 minutes. *Number of sessions*—4 or more sessions. *Total contact time*—longer than 30 minutes.
Program format	Either individual or group counseling may be used. Proactive telephone counseling also is effective. Use of adjuvant self-help material is optional. Followup assessment intervention procedures should be used (see Chapter 6B).
Type of counseling and behavioral therapies	Counseling and behavioral therapies should involve practical counseling (problemsolving/skills-training) (see Table 21) and intra-treatment (see Table 22) and extra-treatment social support (see Table 23).
Pharmacotherapy	Every smoker should be encouraged to use pharmaco-therapies endorsed in this guideline, except in the presence of special circumstances. Special consideration should be given before using pharmacotherapy with selected populations (e.g., pregnancy, adolescents) (see Table 4 for clinical guidelines and Tables 33-39 for specific instructions and precautions). The clinician should explain how these medications increase smoking cessation success and reduce withdrawal symptoms. The first-line pharmacotherapy agents include: bupropion SR, nicotine gum, nicotine inhaler, nicotine nasal spray, and the nicotine patch.
Population	Intensive intervention programs may be used with all tobacco users willing to participate in such efforts.

5 Systems Interventions: Relevance to Health Care Administrators, Insurers, and Purchasers

Background

Traditionally, efforts to increase tobacco intervention in the health care setting have targeted the individual clinician. Such a restricted focus is no longer appropriate. Two considerations argue for expanding the scope of tobacco intervention efforts. First, efforts directed at the individual clinician have yielded disappointing results. For instance, national data suggest that, in a given visit with a clinician, more than one-third of smokers are not advised and assisted with cessation.[11,14,41] Second, an increasing number of Americans today receive their health care in managed care settings. As a consequence, agents such as health system administrators, insurers, and health care purchasers now play a significant role in the health care of most Americans. For example, managed care organizations and other insurers influence medical care through restrictive formularies, performance feedback to clinicians, and marketing approaches that prompt patient demand for particular services.

The influence of health care system administrators, insurers, and purchasers could, in theory, be used to encourage and support the consistent and effective identification and treatment of tobacco users. These agents could craft and implement supportive systems, policies, and environmental prompts that render tobacco use treatment an integral part of health care. Indeed, research clearly shows that systems-level change can reduce smoking prevalence among enrollees of managed health care plans.[66]

Unfortunately, as a society we have not capitalized on the opportunity to use today's health care organizations, insurers, and purchasers to combat tobacco use. For example, treatments for tobacco use (both pharmacotherapy and counseling) are not consistently provided as paid services for subscribers of health insurance packages.[67,68] A recent survey found that only 22 States provided Medicaid coverage for tobacco dependence treatment.[69] Another survey demonstrated that only 39 percent of managed care organizations had partially implemented the recommendations within the original guideline, and only 9 percent had fully implemented the recommendations.[70] This lack of coverage is puzzling given that studies have shown that physician advice to quit is at least as cost-effective as several other preventive medical practices, including the treatment of mild or moderate hypertension or high cholesterol.[71,72] These and other findings resulted in the addition of a new objective to the national health promotion and disease prevention objectives for the year 2000 (*Healthy People 2000*):

Increase to 100 percent the proportion of health plans that offer treatment of nicotine addiction (e.g., tobacco use cessation counseling by health care providers, tobacco use cessation classes, prescriptions for nicotine replacement therapies, and/or other cessation services).[73]

This objective has been modified in *Healthy People 2010* to state:

Increase insurance coverage of evidence-based treatment for nicotine dependency to 100 percent.[74]

In sum, without supportive systems, policies, and environmental prompts, the individual clinician will likely not assess and treat tobacco use consistently. Therefore, just as clinicians must assume responsibility to treat their patients for tobacco use, so must health care administrators, insurers, and purchasers assume responsibility to craft policies, provide resources, and display leadership that results in consistent and effective tobacco use treatment.

Cost-Effectiveness of Smoking Cessation Interventions

Smoking cessation treatments are not only clinically effective, but they are economically defensible as well. It is vital that all three audiences targeted in this guideline recognize that smoking cessation treatments ranging from clinician advice to pharmacotherapy to specialist-delivered intensive programs are cost-effective in relation to other medical interventions.[64] Cost-effectiveness analyses have shown that smoking cessation treatments compare quite favorably with routine medical interventions such as the treatment of hypertension and hypercholesterolemia, and with other preventive interventions such as periodic mammography.[71,75-77] In fact, smoking cessation treatment has been referred to as the "gold standard" of preventive interventions.[78] Smoking cessation treatment remains highly cost-effective, even though a single application of any effective treatment for tobacco dependence may produce sustained abstinence in only a minority of smokers.

The cost-effectiveness of guideline recommendations for smoking cessation is addressed in detail in Chapter 8.

Recommendations for Health Care Administrators, Insurers, and Purchasers

Health care delivery administrators, insurers, and purchasers can promote the treatment of tobacco dependence through a systems approach. Purchasers (often corporations, companies, or other consortia that purchase health care benefits for a group of individuals) should make tobacco assessment and treatment a contractual obligation of the health care insurers and/or providers that sell services to them. In addition to improving the health of their employees or subscribers, mandating coverage for tobacco dependence treatment will result in lower rates of absenteeism[79] and lower utilization of health care resources.[80] Health care administrators and insurers must provide clinicians with assistance to ensure that institutional changes promoting tobacco dependence treatment are implemented universally and systematically. A number of institutional policies would facilitate these interventions such as:

Implementing a tobacco-user identification system in every clinic (Systems Strategy 1).

Providing education, resources, and feedback to promote provider intervention (Systems Strategy 2).

Dedicating staff to provide tobacco dependence treatment and assessing the delivery of this treatment in staff performance evaluations (Systems Strategy 3).

Promoting hospital policies that support and provide tobacco dependence services (Systems Strategy 4).

Including tobacco dependence treatments (both counseling and pharmaco-therapy) identified as effective in this guideline, as paid or covered services for all subscribers or members of health insurance packages (Systems Strategy 5).

Reimbursing clinicians and specialists for delivery of effective tobacco dependence treatments and including these interventions among the defined duties of the clinicians (Systems Strategy 6).

These strategies are based on the evidence described in Chapters 6, 7, and 8, as well as on panel opinion.

Strategies for Health Care Administrators, Insurers, and Purchasers

Systems Strategy 1. Implement a tobacco-user identification system in every clinic

Action	Strategies for implementation	
Implement an office-wide system that ensures that, for EVERY patient at EVERY clinic visit, tobacco-use status is queried and documented.	Office system change:	Expanding the Vital Signs to include tobacco use or implement an alternative universal identification system.
	Responsible staff:	Nurse, medical assistant, receptionist, or other individual already responsible for measuring the vital signs. These staff must be instructed regarding the importance of this activity and serve as non-smoking role models.
	Frequency of utilization:	Every visit for every patient regardless of the reason for the visit.[a]
	System implementation steps:	Prepare progress notepaper or computer records to include tobacco use along with the traditional vital signs for every patient visit. A vital sign stamp also can be used. Alternatives to the vital sign stamp are to place tobacco-use status stickers on all patient charts or to indicate smoking status using computer reminder systems.

> **VITAL SIGNS**
>
> Blood Pressure: _____
>
> Pulse: _____   Weight: _____
>
> Temperature: _____
>
> Respiratory Rate: _____
>
> Tobacco Use: Current   Former   Never
> *(circle one)*

[a] Repeated assessment is *not* necessary in the case of the adult who has never used tobacco or not used tobacco for many years, and for whom this information is clearly documented in the medical record.

Systems Strategy 2. Provide education, resources, and feedback to promote provider intervention

Action	Strategies for implementation
Health care systems should ensure that clinicians have sufficient training to treat tobacco dependence, clinicians and patients have cessation resources, and clinicians are given feedback about their tobacco dependence treatment practices.	*Educate*—On a regular basis, offer lectures/seminars/in-services with CME and/or other credit for tobacco dependence treatment. *Provide resources*—Have patient self-help materials, as well as bupropion SR and nicotine replacement "starter kits," readily available in every examination room. *Report*—Include the provision of tobacco dependence treatment on "report cards" for managed care organizations and other insurers (e.g., NCQA HEDIS). *Provide feedback*—Drawing on data from chart audits, electronic medical records, and computerized patient databases, evaluate the degree to which clinicians are identifying, documenting, and treating patients who use tobacco, and provide feedback to clinicians about their performance.

Systems Strategy 3. Dedicate staff to provide tobacco dependence treatment and assess the delivery of this treatment in staff performance evaluations

Action	Strategies for implementation
Clinical sites should communicate to all staff the importance of intervening with tobacco users and should designate a staff person (e.g., nurse, medical assistant, or other clinician) to coordinate tobacco dependence treatments. Nonphysician personnel may serve as effective, but lower cost, providers of tobacco dependence interventions.	*Designate* a tobacco dependence treatment coordinator for every clinical site. *Delineate* the responsibilities of the tobacco dependence treatment coordinator, including instructing patients on the effective use of treatments (e.g., pharmacotherapy, telephone calls to and from prospective quitters, and scheduled followup visits, especially in the immediate post-quit period). *Communicate* to each staff member (e.g., nurse, physician, medical assistant, pharmacist, or other clinician) his or her responsibilities in the delivery of tobacco dependence services. Incorporate a discussion of these staff responsibilities into training of new and temporary staff.

Systems Strategy 4. Promote hospital policies that support and provide inpatient tobacco dependence services

Action	Strategies for implementation
Provide tobacco dependence treatment to all tobacco users admitted to a hospital.	*Implement* a system to identify and document the tobacco-use status of all hospitalized patients. *Identify* a clinician(s) to deliver tobacco dependence in-patient consultation services for every hospital. *Offer* tobacco dependence treatment to all hospitalized patients who use tobacco. *Reimburse* providers for tobacco dependence in-patient consultation services. *Expand* hospital formularies to include FDA-approved tobacco dependence pharmacotherapies. *Ensure* compliance with JCAHO regulations mandating that all sections of the hospital be entirely smoke-free. *Educate* hospital staff that first-line medications may be used to reduce nicotine withdrawal symptoms, even if the patient is not intending to quit.

Systems Strategy 5. Include tobacco dependence treatments (both counseling and pharmacotherapy) identified as effective in this guideline, as paid or covered services for all subscribers or members of health insurance packages

Action	Strategies for implementation
Provide all insurance subscribers, including MCO members, with coverage for effective tobacco dependence treatments, including pharmacotherapy and counseling.	*Cover*—Include effective tobacco dependence treatments (both counseling and pharmacotherapy) as part of the basic benefits package for all health insurance packages. *Educate*—Inform subscribers, including MCO members, of the availability of covered tobacco dependence treatments (both counseling and pharmacotherapy) and encourage patients to use these services.

Systems Strategy 6. Reimburse clinicians and specialists for delivery of effective tobacco dependence treatments and include these interventions among the defined duties of clinicians

Action	Strategies for implementation
Reimburse fee-for-service clinicians and specialists for delivery of effective tobacco dependence treatments; include tobacco dependence treatments in the defined duties of salaried clinicians and those working in capitated environments.	*Include* tobacco dependence treatment as a reimbursable activity for fee-for-service providers. *Inform* fee-for-service clinicians and specialists that they will be reimbursed for using effective tobacco dependence treatments. *Include* tobacco dependence intervention in the job descriptions and performance evaluations of salaried clinicians and specialists.

6 Evidence

Background

The recommendations summarized in Chapters 2, 3, 4, and 5 are the result of a review and analysis of the extant tobacco cessation literature. The current chapter reports the results of this review and analysis, and describes the efficacy of various treatments, assessments, and strategies for their implementation. This chapter addresses such questions as: Does the professional discipline of the clinician make a difference in the efficacy of the intervention? Are different types of providers effective in delivering interventions? Are minimal interventions, such as clinician advice to quit smoking, effective or are more intensive interventions required? Does the duration of an intervention in number of treatment sessions or in total face-to-face contact time substantially influence efficacy? Are pharmacologic interventions effective, and if so, which ones? Which counseling strategies are particularly helpful? In short, which treatments or assessments are efficacious and how should they be used?

The panel examined the relation between outcomes and 10 major assessment or treatment characteristics or strategies. These 10 characteristic types, and the categories within each, are listed in Table 6. Type of outcome varied across the different characteristics being analyzed. In most analyses, long-term abstinence was the outcome measure, in others it was the rate of smoker identification. The analyses reported in this chapter almost exclusively addressed treatments for cigarette smoking, as opposed to the use of other forms of tobacco, as the small number of studies on the use of noncigarette tobacco products precluded their separate analysis. Finally, the panel attempted to analyze treatment and assessment strategies that constitute distinct approaches that exist in current clinical practice.

The panel chose categories within each characteristic according to three major criteria. First, some categories reflected generally accepted dimensions or taxonomies. An example of this is the categorical nature of the clinician types (physician, psychologist, nurse, and so on). Second, information on the category had to be available in the published literature. Many questions of theoretical interest had to be abandoned simply because the requisite information was not available. Third, the category had to occur with sufficient frequency to permit meaningful statistical analysis. For example, the cut-points of some continuous variables (e.g., total amount of contact time) were determined so there was a sufficient number of studies within each analytical category to permit meaningful analysis.

In ideal circumstances, the panel could evaluate each characteristic by consulting randomized controlled trials relevant to the specific categories in question. Unfortunately, with the exception of pharmacologic interventions, very few or no randomized controlled trials are specifically designed to address the effects of the various categories related to these treatment or assessment characteristics. Moreover, treatment characteristics are frequently confounded with one another. For example, comparisons among clinicians are almost always confounded with the type of counseling and behavioral therapy, format, and intensity of the interventions. Psychologists tend to deliver relatively intensive interventions, whereas physicians tend to deliver brief advice to individuals. Therefore, direct, unconfounded comparisons of categories within a particular

Table 6. Treatment and assessment characteristics analyzed for their relation to abstinence outcomes

Characteristics analyzed	Categories of those characteristics
Screen for tobacco use	No screening system in place. Screening system in place.
Advice to quit	No advice to quit. Physician advice to quit.
Intensity of person-to-person clinical contact	No person-to-person intervention. Minimal counseling (longest session ≤ 3 min in duration). Low intensity counseling (longest session > 3 min and ≤10 min in duration). Higher intensity counseling (longest session > 10 min). Total amount of contact time. Number of person-to-person treatment sessions.
Type of clinician	No clinician. Self-help materials only. Nonphysician health care clinician (e.g., psychologist, counselor, social worker, nurse, dentist, graduate student, pharmacist). Physician. Number of types of clinicians.
Formats of psychosocial intervention	No contact. Self-help/self-administered (e.g., pamphlet, audiotape, videotape, mailed information, computer program). Individual counseling/contact. Group counseling/contact. Proactive telephone counseling/contact. Number of types of formats.
Self-help interventions	Number of self-help interventions. Self-help interventions.

Table 6. Treatment and assessment characteristics analyzed for their relation to abstinence outcomes (continued)

Types of counseling and behavioral therapies	No person-to-person intervention or minimal counseling.
	General—problemsolving/coping skills/relapse prevention/stress management approach.
	Negative affect/depression intervention.
	Weight/diet/nutrition intervention.
	Extra-treatment social support intervention.
	Intra-treatment social support intervention.
	Contingency contracting/instrumental contingencies.
	Rapid smoking.
	Other aversive smoking techniques.
	Cigarette fading/smoking reduction prequit.
	Acupuncture.
Pharmacologic interventions	Placebo pharmacotherapy.
	Bupropion SR.
	Clonidine.
	Nicotine gum.
	Nicotine inhaler.
	Nicotine nasal spray.
	Nicotine patch.
	Nortriptyline.
Combination nicotine replacement therapy	One nicotine replacement therapy.
	Two nicotine replacement therapies.
Over-the-counter pharmacotherapy	Placebo over-the-counter nicotine patch therapy.
	Over-the-counter nicotine patch therapy.

characteristic were often impossible. These characteristics were nevertheless analyzed because of their clinical importance, and because it was possible to reduce confounding by careful selection of studies and by statistical control of some confounding factors.

Additional topics, which did not lend themselves to analysis due to a lack of published long-term abstinence data, yet were important and clinically relevant, were nevertheless considered by the panel through a review of the existing literature. The strength of evidence associated with these recommendations clearly indicate that they are not based on meta-analyzed randomized controlled trials.

The present chapter addresses the 10 treatment and assessment characteristics outlined in Table 6 and is divided into three sections: (A) screening and assessment, (B) treatment structure and intensity, and (C) treatment elements.

For each topic, background information, clinical recommendations, and the basis for those recommendations are provided. As described in Chapter 1, each recommendation was given a strength of evidence classification based on the criteria shown in Table 7. Finally, for some topics, recommendations for further research are provided.

A. Screening and Assessment

Screen for Tobacco Use

Recommendation: All patients should be asked if they use tobacco and should have their tobacco-use status documented on a regular basis. Evidence has shown that this significantly increases rates of clinician intervention. (Strength of Evidence = A)

Recommendation: Clinic screening systems such as expanding the vital signs to include tobacco-use status, or the use of other reminder systems such as chart stickers or computer prompts are essential for the consistent assessment, documentation, and intervention with tobacco use. (Strength of Evidence =B)

A thorough review of articles published since the end-date of the original guideline literature review (December 31, 1994), revealed no studies that met criteria for the screening meta-analyses. Therefore, the panel decided to rely on the meta-analyses from the original guideline to determine the impact of tobacco screening systems. Such screening systems were evaluated in terms of their impact on two outcomes: the rate of tobacco cessation intervention by clinicians, and the rate of cessation by patients who smoke.

Identifying Tobacco Users: Impact on Clinical Intervention. Nine studies met the selection criteria from the original guideline and were analyzed using a

Table 7. Summary of strength of evidence for recommendations

Strength of evidence classification	Criteria
Strength of Evidence = A	Multiple well-designed randomized clinical trials, directly relevant to the recommendation, yielded a consistent pattern of findings.
Strength of Evidence = B	Some evidence from randomized clinical trials supported the recommendation, but the scientific support was not optimal. For instance, few randomized trials existed, the trials that did exist were somewhat inconsistent, or the trials were not directly relevant to the recommendation.
Strength of Evidence = C	Reserved for important clinical situations where the panel achieved consensus on the recommendation in the absence of relevant randomized controlled trials.

random-effects meta-analysis to assess the impact of screening systems on the rate of smoking cessation intervention by clinicians. The results of this meta-analysis are shown in Table 8. Implementing clinic systems designed to increase the assessment and documentation of tobacco use status markedly increases the rate at which clinicians intervene with their patients who smoke.

Identifying Tobacco Users: Impact on Tobacco Cessation. Three studies met the selection criteria from the original guideline and were analyzed using a random-effects meta-analysis to assess the impact of identifying smokers on actual rates of smoking cessation. The results of this meta-analysis are shown in Table 9. These results suggest that having a clinic system in place that identifies smokers results in higher rates of smoking cessation, although this finding was not statistically significant and was based on a small number of studies.

Brief Strategy A1 (see Chapter 3A) and Systems Strategy A1 (see Chapter 5) detail an approach for including tobacco-use status as a vital sign with systematic prompts and reminders. Although the data assessing this intervention were exclusively gathered from cigarette smokers, the panel felt that these results were generalizable to all tobacco users. This approach is designed to produce consistent assessment and documentation of tobacco use. Evidence from controlled trials shows that this approach increases the probability that tobacco use is consistently assessed and documented.[12,81-85]

Future Research

The following topic regarding screening for tobacco use requires additional research:

Additional evidence regarding the impact of screening systems on tobacco abstinence rates.

Table 8. Meta-analysis: Impact of having a tobacco use status identification system in place on rates of clinician intervention with their patients who smoke (n = 9 studies)

Screening system	Number of arms	Estimated odds ratio (95% C.I.)	Estimated intervention rate (95% C.I.)
No screening system in place to identify smoking status (reference group)	9	1.0	38.5
Screening system in place to identify smoking status	9	3.1 (2.2-4.2)	65.6 (58.3-72.6)

Table 9. Meta-analysis: Impact of having a tobacco use status identification system in place on abstinence rates among patients who smoke (n = 3 studies)

Screening system	Number of arms	Estimated odds ratio (95% C.I.)	Estimated abstinence rate (95% C.I.)
No screening system in place to identify smoking status (reference group)	3	1.0	3.1
Screening system in place to identify smoking status	3	2.0 (0.8-4.8)	6.4 (1.3-11.6)

Specialized Assessment

Recommendation: Once a tobacco user is identified and advised to quit, the clinician should assess the patient's willingness to quit at this time. (Strength of Evidence = C)

If the patient is willing to make a quit attempt at this time, interventions identified as effective in this guideline should be initiated. (see Chapter 3A and 4)

If the patient is unwilling to quit at this time, a motivational intervention should be provided. (see Chapter 3B)

Recommendation: Tobacco dependence treatment is effective and should be delivered even if specialized assessments are not used or available. (Strength of Evidence = A)

Every individual entering a health care setting should receive an assessment that determines his or her tobacco use status and interest in quitting. The patient should be asked, "Are you willing to make a quit attempt at this time?" Such an assessment (willing or unwilling) is a necessary first step in treatment. In addition, every patient should be assessed for physical or medical conditions that may affect the use of planned treatments (e.g., pharmacotherapy).

The clinician also may want to perform specialized assessments of individual and environmental attributes that provide information for tailoring treatment and that predict quitting success. Specialized assessments refer to the use of formal instruments (e.g., questionnaires, clinical interviews, or physiologic indices such as carbon monoxide, serum nicotine/cotinine levels, and/or pulmonary function) that may be associated with cessation outcome. Some of the variables targeted by specialized assessments that predict quitting success are listed in Table 10.

Table 10. Variables associated with higher or lower abstinence rates

Variables associated with higher abstinence rates	
Variable	**Examples**
High motivation	Tobacco user reports motivation to quit.
Ready to change	Tobacco user is ready to quit within a 1-month period.
Moderate to high self-efficacy	Tobacco user is confident in his or her ability to quit.
Supportive social network	A smoke-free workplace and home; friends who do not smoke in the quitter's presence.
Variables associated with lower abstinence rates	
Variable	**Examples**
High nicotine dependence	Tobacco user has had severe withdrawal during previous quit attempts, smokes heavily (>20 cigarettes/day), and/or has first cigarette of the day within 30 minutes after waking in the morning.
History of psychiatric comorbidity	Tobacco user has a history of depression, schizophrenia, alcoholism, or other chemical dependency.
High stress level	Stressful life circumstances and/or recent or anticipated major life changes (e.g., divorce, job change, and marriage).

Several considerations should be kept in mind regarding the use of specialized assessments. First, there is little consistent evidence that a smoker's status on a specialized assessment is useful for treatment matching. The one exception is that persons highly nicotine dependent may benefit more from 4 mg as opposed to 2 mg nicotine gum (see Chapter 6C, Pharmacotherapy). More importantly, the panel found that, regardless of their standing on specialized assessments, all smokers have the potential to benefit from cessation interventions. Therefore, delivery of tobacco dependence treatments should not depend on the use of specialized assessments. Finally, tailored interventions based on specialized assessments (e.g., stages of change) do not consistently produce higher long-term quit rates than do nontailored interventions of equal intensity. There do exist, however, some promising studies, which suggest that individualizing self-help materials may be beneficial.[86,87] However, more studies are needed that contrast individualized self-help interventions with nonindividualized interventions of equivalent intensity. In addition, the panel recognizes that some effective interventions, such as general problemsolving (see Chapter 6C, Types of Counseling and Behavioral Therapies), entail treatment tailoring based on a systematic assessment of individual patient characteristics.

The existing evidence suggests that treatment can be effective despite the presence of risk factors for relapse (e.g., severe previous withdrawal, depression, other smokers in the home), but abstinence rates in smokers with these characteristics tend to be lower than rates in those without these characteristics.[88-92]

Future Research

The following topic regarding specialized assessment requires additional research:

Whether treatment adjustment based on specialized assessments can improve long-term abstinence rates.

B. Treatment Structure and Intensity

Advice To Quit Smoking

Recommendation: All *physicians* should strongly advise every patient who smokes to quit because evidence shows that physician advice to quit smoking increases abstinence rates. (Strength of Evidence = A)

Recommendation: All *clinicians* should strongly advise their patients who use tobacco to quit. Although studies have not independently addressed the impact of advice to quit by all types of nonphysician clinicians, it is reasonable to believe that such advice is effective in increasing their patients' long-term quit rates. (Strength of Evidence = B)

A thorough literature review identified no new studies since 1994 that examined the efficacy of advice to quit and that met the inclusion criteria for analysis. Therefore, the panel decided to rely on the analysis from the original guideline. Seven studies were included in the meta-analysis of the efficacy of physician advice to quit smoking. In the studies used in this analysis, the modal length of clinician intervention was 3 minutes or less. Two studies in this analysis used interventions lasting about 5 minutes. Results of the meta-analysis on physician advice are shown in Table 11. This analysis shows that brief physician advice significantly increases long-term smoking abstinence rates.

Physician advice only was examined in the Table 11 meta-analysis because there were too few studies to examine advice delivered by any other types of clinicians. The analysis for total amount of contact time (see Table 13 provided in the following subsection) indicates that minimal counseling (advice) delivered by a variety of clinician types increase long-term abstinence rates. Also, it should be noted that studies have shown that dentists and dental hygienists can be effective in assessing and advising patients who use smokeless/spit tobacco to quit (see Chapter 8). Given the large number of smokers who visit a clinician each year, the potential public health impact of universal advice to quit is substantial.

Table 11. Meta-analysis: Efficacy of and estimated abstinence rates for advice to quit by a physician (n = 7 studies)

Advice	Number of arms	Estimated odds ratio (95% C.I.)	Estimated abstinence rate (95% C.I.)
No advice to quit (reference group)	9	1.0	7.9
Physician advice to quit	10	1.3 (1.1-1.6)	10.2 (8.5-12.0)

Future Research

The following topics regarding advice to quit require additional research:

The efficacy of advice to quit smoking given by specific nonphysician clinicians such as nurses, psychologists, pharmacists, dentists, and dental hygienists.

The cumulative efficacy of combined advice from physicians and nonphysician providers.

Intensity of Clinical Interventions

Recommendation: Minimal interventions lasting less than 3 minutes increase overall tobacco abstinence rates. Every tobacco user should be offered at least a minimal intervention whether or not he or she is referred to an intensive intervention. (Strength of Evidence = A)

Recommendation: There is a strong dose-response relation between the session length of person-to-person contact and successful treatment outcomes. Intensive interventions are more effective than less intensive interventions and should be used whenever possible. (Strength of Evidence = A)

Recommendation: Person-to-person treatment delivered for four or more sessions appears especially effective in increasing abstinence rates. Therefore, if feasible, clinicians should strive to meet four or more times with individuals quitting tobacco use. (Strength of Evidence = A)

These recommendations are supported by three separate analyses, one involving session length, one involving total amount of contact time, and one involving the number of sessions.

Session Length. Forty-three studies met selection criteria for comparisons among various session lengths. Whenever possible, session length was categorized based on the maximum amount of time the clinician spent with a smoker addressing tobacco dependence in a single contact. Minimal counseling interventions were defined as 3 minutes or less, low intensity counseling was defined as greater than 3 minutes to 10 minutes, and higher intensity counseling interventions were defined as greater than 10 minutes. Interventions could involve multiple patient-clinician contacts with the session length determined for coding purposes as the length of time of the longest session. These levels of person-to-person contact were compared with a no-contact reference group involving study conditions where subjects received no person-to-person contact (e.g., self-help-only conditions). There is a dose-response relation between session length and abstinence rates. As Table 12 shows, all three session lengths (minimal counseling, low intensity counseling, and higher intensity counseling) significantly increased abstinence rates over those produced by no-contact conditions. However, there was a clear trend for abstinence rates to increase across these session lengths, with higher intensity counseling producing abstinence rates that were significantly higher than the rates produced by minimal or low intensity counseling.

Total Amount of Contact Time. Thirty-five studies met the selection criteria for the analysis assessing the impact of total contact time. The amount of contact time was calculated from the text as the total time accumulated (the number of sessions multiplied by the session length). When the exact time was not known for minimal and low intensity interventions, they were assigned median lengths of 2 and 6.5 minutes respectively. The total amount of contact time was then categorized as no-contact, 1–3 minutes, 4–30 minutes, 31–90 minutes, 91–300 minutes, and greater than 300 minutes. There is a dose-response relation between total amount of contact time and abstinence rates. As Table 13 shows, any contact time significantly increased abstinence rates over those produced by no-contact. However, there was a clear trend for abstinence rates to increase across contact time, with 31–90 minutes producing abstinence rates that were signifi-

Table 12. Meta-analysis: Efficacy of and estimated abstinence rates for various intensity levels of person-to-person contact (n = 43 studies)

Level of contact	Number of arms	Estimated odds ratio (95% C.I.)	Estimated abstinence rate (95% C.I.)
No contact	30	1.0	10.9
Minimal counseling (< 3 minutes)	19	1.3 (1.01, 1.6)	13.4 (10.9, 16.1)
Low intensity counseling (3 – 10 minutes)	16	1.6 (1.2, 2.0)	16.0 (12.8, 19.2)
Higher intensity counseling (> 10 minutes)	55	2.3 (2.0, 2.7)	22.1 (19.4, 24.7)

Table 13. Meta-analysis: Efficacy of and estimated abstinence rates for total amount of contact time (n = 35 studies)

Total amount of contact time	Number of arms	Estimated odds ratio (95% C.I.)	Estimated abstinence rate (95% C.I.)
No minutes	16	1.0	11.0
1-3 minutes	12	1.4 (1.1, 1.8)	14.4 (11.3, 17.5)
4-30 minutes	20	1.9 (1.5, 2.3)	18.8 (15.6, 22.0)
31-90 minutes	16	3.0 (2.3, 3.8)	26.5 (21.5, 31.4)
91-300 minutes	16	3.2 (2.3, 4.6)	28.4 (21.3, 35.5)
>300 minutes	15	2.8 (2.0, 3.9)	25.5 (19.2, 31.7)

cantly higher than the rates produced by 1–3 minutes of total contact time. There was no evidence that more than 90 minutes of contact time increases abstinence rates further.

Number of Sessions. Forty-five studies involving at least some person-to-person contact met selection criteria for the analysis addressing the impact of number of treatment sessions. The number of treatment sessions was categorized as zero or one session, two to three sessions, four to eight sessions, and greater than eight sessions. Zero or one session was used as the reference group. As shown in Table 14, multiple treatment sessions increase smoking abstinence rates over those produced by zero or one session. The evidence suggests a dose-response relation between number of sessions and treatment efficacy, with treatments lasting more than 8 sessions significantly more effective than interventions lasting either zero to one or two to three sessions.

Future Research

The following topics regarding intensity of person-to-person contact require additional research:

The effects of treatment duration and spacing of sessions (i.e., the number of days or weeks over which treatment is spread). For instance, does front-loading sessions (having the majority of the sessions during the first few weeks of a quit attempt), or spacing sessions throughout the quit attempt yield better long-term abstinence rates?

Methods to increase the patient utilization and completion of intensive treatments.

Efficacy of intensive inpatient treatment programs.

Table 14. Meta-analysis: Efficacy of and estimated abstinence rates for number of person-to-person treatment sessions (n = 45 studies)

Number of sessions	Number of arms	Estimated odds ratio (95% C.I.)	Estimated abstinence rate (95% C.I.)
0-1 session	43	1.0	12.4
2-3 sessions	17	1.4 (1.1, 1.7)	16.3 (13.7, 19.0)
4-8 sessions	23	1.9 (1.6, 2.2)	20.9 (18.1, 23.6)
> 8 sessions	51	2.3 (2.1, 3.0)	24.7 (21.0, 28.4)

Type of Clinician

Recommendation: Treatment delivered by a variety of clinician types increases abstinence rates. Therefore, all clinicians should provide smoking cessation interventions. (Strength of Evidence = A)

Recommendation: Treatments delivered by multiple types of clinicians are more effective than interventions delivered by a single type of clinician. Therefore, if feasible, the delivery of interventions by more than one type of clinician is encouraged. (Strength of Evidence = C)

Clinician Types. Twenty-nine studies met selection criteria for the analysis examining the effectiveness of various types of clinicians providing smoking cessation interventions. These analyses compared the efficacy of interventions delivered by specific types of clinicians with interventions where there were no clinicians (e.g., where there was no intervention or the intervention consisted of self-help materials only). Smoking cessation interventions delivered by any single type of health care provider, such as a physician or nonphysician clinician (e.g., psychologist, nurse, dentist, or counselor), or by multiple clinicians, increase abstinence rates relative to interventions where there is no clinician (e.g., self-help interventions). None of the studies in these analyses involved pharmacotherapy, but they did involve psychosocial intervention of varying intensities. Results are shown in Table 15. Results are consistent across diverse clinician groups, with no clear advantage to any single clinician type.

Number of Clinician Types. Thirty-seven studies met selection criteria for the analysis examining the effectiveness of multiple clinicians used in smoking cessation interventions. Please note that "multiple clinicians" refers to the number of different types of clinicians, not the number of total clinicians regardless of type. The latter information was rarely available from the study reports. Smoking cessation interventions delivered by multiple types of clinicians increase abstinence rates relative to those produced by interventions where there is no clinician. Results are shown in Table 16. The data displayed in Table 16 also show a nonsignificant trend for multiple types of clinicians to be more efficacious than a

Table 15. Meta-analysis: Efficacy of and estimated abstinence rates for interventions delivered by various types of clinicians (n = 29 studies)

Type of clinician	Number of arms	Estimated odds ratio (95% C.I.)	Estimated abstinence rate (95% C.I.)
No clinician	16	1.0	10.2
Self-help	47	1.1 (0.9, 1.3)	10.9 (9.1, 12.7)
Nonphysician clinician	39	1.7 (1.3, 2.1)	15.8 (12.8, 18.8)
Physician clinician	11	2.2 (1.5, 3.2)	19.9 (13.7, 26.2)

single clinician type. This suggests that a variety of clinicians, including physician clinicians, and nonphysician clinicians, such as nurses, dentists, dental hygienists, psychologists, pharmacists, and health educators, can play an important role in promoting smoking cessation.

Future Research

The following topics regarding type of clinician require additional research:

The effectiveness of specific types of clinicians, such as nurses, physician assistants, pharmacists, social workers, etc.

The relative effectiveness of various numbers and types of clinicians, with the intensity of the intervention held constant.

Strategies to integrate tobacco dependence treatment across diverse disciplines and settings.

Table 16. Meta-analysis: Efficacy of and estimated abstinence rates for interventions delivered by various numbers of clinician types (n = 37 studies)

Number of clinician types	Number of arms	Estimated odds ratio (95% C.I.)	Estimated abstinence rate (95% C.I.)
No clinician	30	1.0	10.8
One clinician type	50	1.8 (1.5, 2.2)	18.3 (15.4, 21.1)
Two clinician types	16	2.5 (1.9, 3.4)	23.6 (18.4, 28.7)
Three or more clinician types	7	2.4 (2.1, 2.9)	23.0 (20.0, 25.9)

Formats of Psychosocial Treatments _____

Recommendation: Proactive telephone counseling, group counseling, and individual counseling formats are effective and should be used in smoking cessation interventions. (Strength of Evidence = A)

Recommendation: Smoking cessation interventions that are delivered in multiple formats increase abstinence rates and should be encouraged. (Strength of Evidence = A)

Format Types. Fifty-eight studies met selection criteria and were included in the analysis comparing different types of formats. Smoking cessation interventions delivered by means of proactive telephone counseling/contact, individual counseling, and group counseling/contact all increase abstinence rates relative to no intervention.

This format meta-analysis also evaluated the efficacy of self-help interventions (e.g., pamphlets/booklets/mailings/manuals, videotapes, audiotapes, referrals to 12-step programs, mass media community level interventions, reactive telephone hotlines/helplines, computer programs/Internet, and lists of community programs). Interventions delivered by means of widely varied self-help materials (whether as stand-alone treatments or as adjuvants) appear to increase abstinence rates relative to no intervention in this particular analysis. However, the effect of self-help is weak and inconsistent across analyses conducted for this guideline. The impact of self-help is certainly smaller and less certain than that of proactive telephone, individual, or group counseling. Results of this analysis are shown in Table 17.

Number of Formats. Fifty-four studies met selection criteria and were included in the analysis comparing the number of format types used for smoking cessation interventions. The self-help treatments included in this analysis occurred either by themselves or as adjuvants to other treatments. Smoking cessation interventions that used more than two format types were more effective than interventions that used a single format type. Results of this analysis are shown in Table 18.

Self-help: focused analyses. Because the format analysis revealed self-help to be of marginal efficacy, another analysis was undertaken to provide additional, focused information on self-help. Studies were accepted for this analysis if the presence of self-help materials constituted the sole difference in treatment arms. In the main format analysis, some treatment arms differed on factors other than self-help per se (e.g., intensity of adjuvant counseling). The treatments that accompanied self-help material in the focused analysis ranged from no advice or counseling to intensive counseling. The results of this analysis were comparable to those in the larger format analysis (i.e., self-help was of marginal efficacy).

Twenty-one studies met selection criteria to evaluate the efficacy of providing multiple types of self-help interventions (e.g., pamphlets, videotapes, audiotapes, and reactive hotlines/helplines). The results provide little evidence that the

Table 17. Meta-analysis: Efficacy of and estimated abstinence rates for various types of format (n = 58 studies)

Format	Number of arms	Estimated odds ratio (95% C.I.)	Estimated abstinence rate (95% C.I.)
No format	20	1.0	10.8
Self-help	93	1.2 (1.02, 1.3)	12.3 (10.9, 13.6)
Proactive telephone counseling	26	1.2 (1.1, 1.4)	13.1 (11.4, 14.8)
Group counseling	52	1.3 (1.1, 1.6)	13.9 (11.6, 16.1)
Individual counseling	67	1.7 (1.4, 2.0)	16.8 (14.7, 19.1)

provision of multiple types of self-help, when offered without any person-to-person intervention, significantly enhances treatment outcomes (see Table 19).

There are two limitations to interpreting these results. First, self-help materials vary greatly in nature and intensity. It is possible that some sub-types of self-help are, in fact, efficacious (e.g., those that are individualized). Second, a large number of smokers report that they quit on their own without clinical support or contact.[93] The extent to which use of self-help materials aids self-quitters was not addressed in guideline analyses.

The previous analyses failed to show a consistent, beneficial effect due to self-help. Two final meta-analyses addressed the impact of self-help brochures per se. In one analysis, brochures were used as the only intervention. In the other analysis, self-help brochures were used as adjuvants to counseling. In neither analysis did self-help significantly boost abstinence rates.

Table 18. Meta-analysis: Efficacy of and estimated abstinence rates for number of formats (n = 54 studies)

Number of formats[a]	Number of arms	Estimated odds ratio (95% C.I.)	Estimated abstinence rate (95% C.I.)
No format	20	1.0	10.8
One format	51	1.5 (1.2, 1.8)	15.1 (12.8, 17.4)
Two formats	55	1.9 (1.6, 2.2)	18.5 (15.8, 21.1)
Three or four formats	19	2.5 (2.1, 3.0)	23.2 (19.9, 26.6)

[a] Formats included self-help, proactive telephone counseling, group, or individual counseling.

Table 19. Meta-analysis: Efficacy of and estimated abstinence rates for number of types of self-help (n = 21 studies)

Factor	Number of arms	Estimated odds ratio (95% C.I.)	Estimated abstinence rate (95% C.I.)
No self-help	17	1.0	14.3
One type of self-help	27	1.0 (0.9, 1.1)	14.4 (12.9, 15.9)
Two or more types	10	1.1 (0.9, 1.5)	15.7 (12.3, 19.2)

Future Research

The following topics regarding formats require additional research:

Identify which combinations of formats are effective.

The efficacy of innovative approaches to self-help such as individualized computerized interventions.[87,94,95]

The efficacy of reactive telephone hotlines/helplines.[60,96-99]

The relative efficacy of different types of self-help interventions.

The efficacy of self-help materials as adjuvant treatments. Do they add significantly to the effectiveness of other proven tobacco dependence treatments such as individual counseling, group counseling, proactive telephone counseling, and pharmacotherapy?

Followup Assessment and Procedures

Recommendation: All patients who receive a tobacco dependence intervention should be assessed for abstinence at the completion of treatment and during subsequent clinic contacts. (1) Abstinent patients should receive relapse prevention treatment (see Chapter 3C, For the Patient Who Has Quit). (2) Patients who have relapsed should be assessed to determine whether they are willing to make another quit attempt. (Strength of Evidence = C):

If the patient is willing to make another quit attempt, provide or arrange additional treatment (see Chapter 3A, For the Patient Willing To Quit).

If the patient is not willing to try to quit, provide an intervention to promote motivation to quit (see Chapter 3B, For the Patient Unwilling To Quit).

All patients should be assessed with respect to their smoking status during all followup tobacco dependence contacts. In particular, assessments within the first week after quitting also should be encouraged.[100] Abstinent patients should receive relapse prevention treatment (see Chapter 3C, Brief Strategy C1 and Brief Strategy C2) including reinforcement for their decision to quit, congratulations on their success at quitting, and encouragement to remain abstinent.[62] Clinicians also should inquire about current and future threats to abstinence and provide appropriate suggestions for coping with these threats.

Patients who have relapsed should again be assessed for their willingness to quit. Patients who are currently motivated to make another quit attempt should be provided with a tobacco dependence intervention (see Chapter 3A, For the Patient Willing To Quit). Clinicians may wish to increase the intensity of psychosocial treatment at this time or refer the patient to a tobacco dependence specialist/program for a more intensive treatment if the patient is willing. In addition, pharmacotherapy should be again offered to the patient. If the previous cessation attempt included pharmacotherapy, the clinician should review whether the patient used these medications in an effective manner and determine whether the medication was helpful. Based on this assessment, recommend retreatment with the same pharmacotherapy, another pharmacotherapy, or combination nicotine replacement therapies (see Tables 33-39).

Patients who are unwilling to quit at the current time should receive a brief intervention designed to promote the motivation to quit (see Chapter 3B, Brief Strategy B. Enhancing motivation to quit tobacco—the "5 R's").

Future Research

The following topics regarding followup assessment require additional research:

The optimal timing and types of relapse prevention interventions.

The efficacy of various formats for relapse prevention treatments. For instance, are telephone contacts effective in reducing the likelihood of relapse after a minimal intervention?

C. Treatment Elements

Types of Counseling and Behavioral Therapies

Recommendation: Three types of counseling and behavioral therapies result in higher abstinence rates: (1) providing smokers with practical counseling (problemsolving skills/skills training); (2) providing social support as part of treatment; and (3) helping smokers obtain social support outside of treatment. These types of counseling and behavioral therapies should be included in smoking cessation interventions. (Strength of Evidence = B)

Recommendation: Aversive smoking interventions (rapid smoking, rapid puffing, other aversive smoking techniques) increase abstinence rates and may be used with smokers who desire such treatment or who have been unsuccessful using other interventions. (Strength of Evidence = B)

Sixty-two studies met selection criteria for analyses examining the effectiveness of interventions using various types of counseling and behavioral therapies. The results, shown in Table 20, reveal that four specific types of counseling and behavioral therapy categories yield statistically significant increases in abstinence rates relative to no-contact (e.g., untreated control conditions). These categories are: (1) providing practical counseling such as problemsolving/skills training/relapse prevention/stress management; (2) providing support during a smoker's direct contact with a clinician (intra-treatment social support); (3) intervening to increase social support in the smoker's environment (extra-treatment social support); and (4) using aversive smoking procedures (rapid smoking, rapid puffing, other smoking exposure). A separate analysis was conducted eliminating studies that included the use of FDA-approved pharmacotherapies. The results of this analysis were substantially similar to the main analysis.

Table 20. Meta-analysis: Efficacy of and estimated abstinence rates for various types of counseling and behavioral therapies (n = 62 studies)

Type of counseling and behavioral therapy	Number of arms	Estimated odds ratio (95% C.I.)	Estimated abstinence rate (95% C.I.)
No counseling/ behavioral therapy	35	1.0	11.2
Relaxation/breathing	31	1.0 (0.7, 1.3)	10.8 (7.9, 13.8)
Contingency contracting	22	1.0 (0.7, 1.4)	11.2 (7.8, 14.6)
Weight/diet	19	1.0 (0.8, 1.3)	11.2 (8.5, 14.0)
Cigarette fading	25	1.1 (0.8, 1.5)	11.8 (8.4, 15.3)
Negative affect	8	1.2 (0.8, 1.9)	13.6 (8.7, 18.5)
Intra-treatment social support	50	1.3 (1.1, 1.6)	14.4 (12.3, 16.5)
Extra-treatment social support	19	1.5 (1.1, 2.1)	16.2 (11.8, 20.6)
General – problemsolving	104	1.5 (1.3, 1.8)	16.2 (14.0, 18.5)
Other aversive smoking	19	1.7 (1.04, 2.8)	17.7 (11.2, 24.9)
Rapid smoking	19	2.0 (1.1, 3.5)	19.9 (11.2, 29.0)

The strength of evidence for the recommendations regarding types of counseling and behavioral therapy categories did not warrant an "A" rating for several reasons. First, smoking cessation interventions rarely used a particular type of counseling or behavioral therapy in isolation. Second, various types of counseling and behavioral therapies tended to be correlated with other treatment characteristics. For instance, some types of counseling and behavioral therapies were more likely to be delivered using a greater number of sessions across longer time periods. Third, it must be noted that all of these types of counseling and behavioral therapies were compared with no-contact/control conditions. Therefore, the control conditions in this meta-analysis did not control for nonspecific or placebo effects of treatment. This further restricted the ability to attribute efficacy to particular types of counseling and behavioral therapies, per se. Fourth, the studies used in this analysis often tailored the types of counseling and behavioral therapies to the needs of special populations being studied, thereby affecting the generalizability of the study results. Fifth, there was considerable heterogeneity within each type of counseling and behavioral therapy.

In the types of counseling and behavioral therapies meta-analysis, six studies examined the effect of dieting and physical activity interventions on smoking cessation. Although dieting and physical activity did not significantly increase abstinence rates based on that analysis, a single recent study published after the date for inclusion in meta-analysis found that vigorous exercise did boost quit rates.[101]

The treatments targeting negative affect were administered both to general populations as well as to special populations (e.g., smokers with a history of depression).[102,103] It is possible that different results would have been found if the study arms were restricted to smokers at risk for negative affect.

Tables 21, 22, and 23 outline elements of practical counseling (problemsolving/skills training), intra-treatment social support, and extra-treatment social support respectively. These tables are designed to help clinicians using these counseling and behavioral therapies. It must be noted, however, that these treatment labels are nonspecific and include heterogeneous treatment elements.

Another type of behavioral therapy associated with superior outcomes is aversive smoking. This involves sessions of guided smoking where the patient smokes intensively, often to the point of discomfort, malaise, nausea, and/or vomiting. Some aversive smoking techniques, such as rapid smoking, may constitute a health risk and should be conducted only with appropriate medical screening and supervision. Aversive smoking interventions are infrequently used today.

Acupuncture. A separate meta-analysis was conducted for acupuncture. This analysis was conducted to achieve a sensitive test on the small body of studies that use this technique. Evidence, as shown in Table 24, did not support the efficacy of acupuncture as a smoking cessation treatment. The acupuncture meta-analysis comparing "active" acupuncture with "control" acupuncture revealed no difference in efficacy between the two types of procedures. These results suggest that any effect of acupuncture might be produced by factors such as positive expectations about the procedure.

Table 21. Common elements of practical counseling (problemsolving/ skills training)

Practical counseling (problemsolving/ skills training) treatment component	Examples
Recognize danger situations—Identify events, internal states, or activities that increase the risk of smoking or relapse.	■ Negative affect. ■ Being around other smokers. ■ Drinking alcohol. ■ Experiencing urges. ■ Being under time pressure.
Develop coping skills—Identify and practice coping or problemsolving skills. Typically, these skills are intended to cope with danger situations.	■ Learning to anticipate and avoid temptation. ■ Learning cognitive strategies that will reduce negative moods. ■ Accomplishing lifestyle changes that reduce stress, improve quality of life, or produce pleasure. ■ Learning cognitive and behavioral activities to cope with smoking urges (e.g., distracting attention).
Provide basic information—provide basic information about smoking and successful quitting.	■ The fact that any smoking (even a single puff) increases the likelihood of a full relapse. ■ Withdrawal typically peaks within 1-3 weeks after quitting. ■ Withdrawal symptoms include negative mood, urges to smoke, and difficulty concentrating. ■ The addictive nature of smoking.

Hypnosis. The original guideline did not conduct a separate meta-analysis on hypnosis because few studies met inclusion criteria, and those that did used very heterogeneous hypnotic procedures. There was no common or standard intervention technique to analyze. Literature screening for the updated guideline revealed no new published studies on the treatment of tobacco dependence by hypnosis that met the inclusion criteria; therefore, this topic did not warrant re-examination. Moreover, an independent review of hypnotherapy trials by the Cochrane Group found insufficient evidence to support hypnosis as a treatment for smoking cessation.[104]

Other Interventions. There were insufficient studies to address the efficacy of other types of counseling and behavioral therapies such as physiological feedback and restricted environmental stimulation therapy.

Table 22. Common elements of intra-treatment supportive interventions

Supportive treatment component	Examples
Encourage the patient in the quit attempt.	■ Note that effective tobacco dependence treatments are now available. ■ Note that one-half of all people who have ever smoked have now quit. ■ Communicate belief in patient's ability to quit.
Communicate caring and concern.	■ Ask how patient feels about quitting. ■ Directly express concern and willingness to help. ■ Be open to the patient's expression of fears of quitting, difficulties experienced, and ambivalent feelings.
Encourage the patient to talk about the quitting process.	**Ask about:** ■ Reasons the patient wants to quit. ■ Concerns or worries about quitting. ■ Success the patient has achieved. ■ Difficulties encountered while quitting.

Table 23. Common elements of extra-treatment supportive interventions

Supportive treatment component	Examples
Train patient in support solicitation skills	■ Show videotapes that model support skills. ■ Practice requesting social support from family, friends, and coworkers. ■ Aid patient in establishing a smoke-free home.
Prompt support seeking	■ Help patient identify supportive others. ■ Call the patient to remind him or her to seek support. ■ Inform patients of community resources such as hotlines and helplines.
Clinician arranges outside support	■ Mail letters to supportive others. ■ Call supportive others. ■ Invite others to cessation sessions. ■ Assign patients to be "buddies" for one another.

Table 24. Meta-analysis: Efficacy of and estimated abstinence rates for acupuncture (n = 5 studies)

Treatment	Number of arms	Estimated odds ratio (95% C.I.)	Estimated abstinence rate (95% C.I.)
Placebo	7	1.0	8.3
Acupuncture	8	1.1 (0.7, 1.6)	8.9 (5.5, 12.3)

Future Research

The following topics regarding types of counseling and behavioral therapies require additional research:

Motivational interventions, cigarette fading, hypnosis, physiological feedback of smoking impacts, 12-step models, and restricted environmental stimulation therapy.

Mechanisms through which counseling interventions exert their effects.

Efficacy of specific counseling interventions among various patient populations (e.g., those with cancers, chronic obstructive pulmonary disease (COPD), and atherosclerosis).

Alternative Treatment Models for the Treatment of Tobacco Dependence—Stepped Care and Individual Tailoring

The panel concluded that there is not enough evidence to propose a recommendation regarding: (1) a stepped-care model for delivery of tobacco dependence treatment; and (2) individually tailored interventions (e.g., using the transtheoretical model). Both of these intervention strategies hold promise, and enjoy some empirical support. Tailored self-help approaches especially enjoy some support.[105-107] Unfortunately, there is insufficient data to indicate that either approach yields a significant incremental impact on long-term abstinence rates over the impact of nontailored counseling approaches of similar intensity. As a result, there needs to be additional research to test the efficacy of these strategies. Some of the needed research includes:

Whether the use of stepped-care intervention strategies improves long-term abstinence rates.

Whether the use of treatment matching strategies improves long-term abstinence rates.

Whether the use of tailored intervention strategies improves long-term abstinence rates.

Whether targeted reductions in the number of cigarettes smoked per day increases long-term rates of abstinence.[108]

Whether staged-based treatments developed in keeping with the transtheoretical model significantly improve long-term abstinence rates relative to comparably intense, alternative counseling strategies (e.g., where patients receive only a standard motivational treatment or cessation treatment depending on their willingness to quit).

Pharmacotherapy

Recommendation: All patients attempting to quit should be encouraged to use effective pharmacotherapies for smoking cessation except in the presence of special circumstances. (Strength of Evidence = A)

Recommendation: Long-term smoking cessation pharmacotherapy should be considered as a strategy to reduce the likelihood of relapse. (Strength of Evidence = C)

As with other chronic diseases, the most effective treatment of tobacco dependence requires the use of multiple modalities. Pharmacotherapy is a vital element of a multicomponent approach. The clinician should encourage all patients initiating a quit attempt to use one or a combination of efficacious pharmacotherapies, although pharmacotherapy use requires special consideration with some patient groups (e.g., those with medical contraindications, those smoking fewer than 10 cigarettes a day, pregnant/breastfeeding women and adolescent smokers). The guideline panel identified five first-line medications (bupropion SR, nicotine gum, nicotine inhaler, nicotine nasal spray, and the nicotine patch) and two second-line medications (clonidine and nortriptyline) for smoking cessation. Each has been documented to increase significantly rates of long-term smoking abstinence. No other pharmacotherapeutic treatments were supported by a consistent body of scientific evidence.

The pharmacotherapy meta-analyses were designed to compare particular pharmacotherapies with the placebo controls in each study. Because of substantial differences across the studies evaluating the different types of pharmacotherapies, it is inappropriate to compare the results for one medication with those for another in the tables that follow.

Pharmacotherapy meta-analyses included predominately studies with "self-selected" populations. In addition, in pharmacotherapy studies both experimental and control subjects typically received substantial counseling. Both of these factors tend to produce higher abstinence rates in reference or placebo subjects than are typically observed among self-quitters.

Recommendations Regarding Specific Pharmacotherapies: First-Line Medications

First-line pharmacotherapies have been found to be safe and effective for tobacco dependence treatment and have been approved by the U.S. Food and Drug Administration (FDA) for this use. First-line medications have established empirical record of efficacy, and should be considered first as part of tobacco dependence treatment except in cases of contraindications.

The listing of the first-line medications is provided alphabetically. Meta-analyses did not contrast the relative efficacy of these medications.

Bupropion SR (Sustained Release Bupropion) _____

Recommendation: Bupropion SR is an efficacious smoking cessation treatment that patients should be encouraged to use. (Strength of Evidence = A)

Two large multicenter studies met selection criteria and were included in the analysis comparing bupropion sustained release (SR) to placebo. Results of this analysis are shown in Table 25. As can be seen from this analysis, the use of bupropion SR approximately doubles long-term abstinence rates when compared to a placebo.

Bupropion SR is the first non-nicotine medication shown to be effective for smoking cessation and approved by the FDA for that use. Its mechanism of action is presumed to be mediated by its capacity to block neural re-uptake of dopamine and/or norepinephrine. It is contraindicated in patients with a seizure disorder, a current or prior diagnosis of bulimia or anorexia nervosa, use of a monoamine oxidase (MAO) inhibitor within the previous 14 days, or in patients on another medication that contains bupropion. Bupropion SR can be used in combination with nicotine replacement therapies. Bupropion SR is available exclusively as a prescription medication both with an indication for smoking cessation (Zyban) and an indication for depression (Wellbutrin). Suggestions regarding the clinical use of bupropion SR are provided in Table 33.

Table 25. Meta-analysis: Efficacy of and estimated abstinence rates for bupropion SR (n = 2 studies)

Pharmacotherapy	Number of arms	Estimated odds ratio (95% C.I.)	Estimated abstinence rate (95% C.I.)
Placebo	2	1.0	17.3
Bupropion SR	4	2.1 (1.5, 3.0)	30.5 (23.2, 37.8)

Nicotine Gum

Recommendation: Nicotine gum is an efficacious smoking cessation treatment that patients should be encouraged to use. (Strength of Evidence = A)

Recommendation: Clinicians should offer 4 mg rather than 2 mg nicotine gum to highly dependent smokers. (Strength of Evidence = B)

Thirteen studies met selection criteria and were included in the analysis comparing nicotine gum to placebo. Results of this analysis are shown in Table 26. As can be seen by the estimated odds ratio from this analysis, 2 mg nicotine gum improves long-term abstinence rates by approximately 30–80 percent as compared with placebo. Furthermore, a close review of the literature suggests that the 4 mg gum is more efficacious than the 2 mg gum as an aid to smoking cessation in highly dependent smokers (see Table 10. Variables associated with higher or lower abstinence rates).[109,110]

Nicotine gum is currently available exclusively as an over-the-counter medication and is packaged with important instructions on correct usage, including chewing instructions. Suggestions regarding the clinical use of nicotine gum are provided in Table 34.

Nicotine Inhaler

Recommendation: The nicotine inhaler is an efficacious smoking cessation treatment that patients should be encouraged to use. (Strength of Evidence = A)

Four studies met selection criteria and were included in the analysis comparing the nicotine inhaler to placebo. Results of this analysis are shown in Table 27. As can be seen from this analysis, the nicotine inhaler more than doubles long-term abstinence rates when compared to a placebo inhaler.

The nicotine inhaler is available exclusively as a prescription medication. Suggestions regarding the clinical use of the nicotine inhaler are provided in Table 35.

Table 26. Meta-analysis: Efficacy of and estimated abstinence rates for 2 mg nicotine gum (n = 13 studies)

Pharmacotherapy	Number of arms	Estimated odds ratio (95% C.I.)	Estimated abstinence rate (95% C.I.)
Placebo	16	1.0	17.1
Nicotine gum	18	1.5 (1.3, 1.8)	23.7 (20.6, 26.7)

Table 27. Meta-analysis: Efficacy of and estimated abstinence rates for nicotine inhaler (n = 4 studies)

Pharmacotherapy	Number of arms	Estimated odds ratio (95% C.I.)	Estimated abstinence rate (95% C.I.)
Placebo	4	1.0	10.5
Nicotine inhaler	4	2.5 (1.7, 3.6)	22.8 (16.4, 29.2)

Nicotine Nasal Spray

Recommendation: Nicotine nasal spray is an efficacious smoking cessation treatment that patients should be encouraged to use. (Strength of Evidence = A)

Three studies met selection criteria and were included in the analysis comparing nicotine nasal spray to placebo. Results of this analysis are shown in Table 28. As can be seen from this analysis, nicotine nasal spray more than doubles long-term abstinence rates when compared to a placebo spray.

Nicotine nasal spray is available exclusively as a prescription medication. Suggestions regarding the clinical use of the nicotine nasal spray are provided in Table 36.

Nicotine Patch

Recommendation: The nicotine patch is an efficacious smoking cessation treatment that patients should be encouraged to use. (Strength of Evidence = A)

Twenty-seven studies met selection criteria and were included in the analysis comparing the nicotine patch to placebo. Results of this analysis are shown in Table 29. As can be seen from this analysis, the nicotine patch approximately doubles long-term abstinence rates over those produced by placebo interventions.

The nicotine patch is available both as an over-the-counter medication and as a prescription medication. Suggestions regarding clinical use of the nicotine patch are provided in Table 37.

Table 28. Meta-analysis: Efficacy of and estimated abstinence rates for nicotine nasal spray (n = 3 studies)

Pharmacotherapy	Number of arms	Estimated odds ratio (95% C.I.)	Estimated abstinence rate (95% C.I.)
Placebo	3	1.0	13.9
Nicotine nasal spray	3	2.7 (1.8, 4.1)	30.5 (21.8, 39.2)

Table 29. Meta-analysis: Efficacy of and estimated abstinence rates for the nicotine patch (n = 27 studies)

Pharmacotherapy	Number of arms	Estimated odds ratio (95% C.I.)	Estimated abstinence rate (95% C.I.)
Placebo	28	1.0	10.0
Nicotine patch	32	1.9 (1.7, 2.2)	17.7 (16.0, 19.5)

Recommendations Regarding Specific Pharmacotherapies: Second-Line Medications

Second-line medications are pharmacotherapies for which there is evidence of efficacy for treating tobacco dependence, but they have a more limited role than first-line medications because: (1) the FDA has not approved them for a tobacco dependence treatment indication; and (2) there are more concerns about potential side effects than exist with first-line medications. Second-line treatments should be considered for use on a case-by-case basis after first-line treatments have been used or considered.

The listing of the second-line medications is provided alphabetically. Meta-analyses did not contrast the relative efficacy of these medications.

Clonidine

Recommendation: Clonidine is an efficacious smoking cessation treatment. It may be used under a physician's supervision as a second-line agent to treat tobacco dependence. (Strength of Evidence = A)

Five studies met selection criteria and were included in the analysis comparing clonidine to placebo. Results of this analysis are shown in Table 30. As can be seen from this analysis, the use of clonidine approximately doubles abstinence rates when compared to a placebo. These studies varied the clonidine dose from 0.1 to 0.75 mg/day. The drug was delivered either transdermally or orally. It should be noted that abrupt discontinuation of clonidine can result in symptoms

Table 30. Meta-analysis: Efficacy of and estimated abstinence rates for clonidine (n = 5 studies)

Pharmacotherapy	Number of arms	Estimated odds ratio (95% C.I.)	Estimated abstinence rate (95% C.I.)
Placebo	6	1.0	13.9
Clonidine	8	2.1 (1.4, 3.2)	25.6 (17.7, 33.6)

such as nervousness, agitation, headache, and tremor, accompanied or followed by a rapid rise in blood pressure and elevated catecholamine levels.

Clonidine is used primarily as an antihypertensive medication and has not been approved by the FDA as a smoking cessation medication. Therefore, clinicians need to be aware of the specific warnings regarding this medication as well as its side-effect profile.

Additionally, a specific dosing regimen for the use of clonidine has not been established. Because of the warnings associated with clonidine discontinuation, the variability in dosages used to test this medication, and a lack of FDA approval, the guideline panel chose to recommend clonidine as a second-line agent. As such, clonidine should be considered for smoking cessation under a physician's direction with patients unable to use first-line medications because of contraindications or with patients who were unable to quit using first-line medications. Suggestions regarding clinical use of clonidine are provided in Table 38.

Nortriptyline

Recommendation: Nortriptyline is an efficacious smoking cessation treatment. It may be used under a physician's supervision as a second-line agent to treat tobacco dependence. (Strength of Evidence = B)

Two studies met selection criteria and were included in the analysis comparing nortriptyline to placebo. Results of this analysis are shown in Table 31. As can be seen from this analysis, the use of nortriptyline increases abstinence rates when compared to a placebo.

Nortriptyline is used primarily as an antidepressant and has not been evaluated or approved by the FDA as a smoking cessation medication. Clinicians need to be aware of the specific warnings regarding this medication as well as its side-effect profile. Because of the limited number of studies examining nortriptyline and the small sample sizes within those studies, the guideline panel determined that the recommendation warranted a strength of evidence equal to B. Because of this strength of evidence, the side-effect profile, and the lack of FDA approval for tobacco dependence treatment, nortriptyline is recommended as a second-line agent. As such, nortriptyline should be considered for smoking cessation under a physician's direction with patients unable to use first-line medications because of

Table 31. Meta-analysis: Efficacy of and estimated abstinence rates for nortriptyline (n = 2 studies)

Pharmacotherapy	Number of arms	Estimated odds ratio (95% C.I.)	Estimated abstinence rate (95% C.I.)
Placebo	3	1.0	11.7
Nortriptyline	3	3.2 (1.8, 5.7)	30.1 (18.1, 41.6)

contraindications or with patients who were unable to quit using first-line medications. Suggestions regarding clinical use of nortriptyline are provided in Table 39.

Combination Nicotine Replacement Therapy _____

Recommendation: Combining the nicotine patch with a self-administered form of nicotine replacement therapy (either the nicotine gum or nicotine nasal spray) is more efficacious than a single form of nicotine replacement, and patients should be encouraged to use such combined treatments if they are unable to quit using a single type of first-line pharmacotherapy. (Strength of Evidence = B)

Three studies met selection criteria for the combination nicotine replacement therapy (NRT) meta-analysis. This analysis was intended to address the hypothesis that combination pharmacotherapy is more effective than monotherapy (the use of a single pharmacotherapy) if the combination therapy comprises two different types of pharmacotherapy. Specifically, the hypothesis holds that one type of pharmacotherapy should involve passive dosing that produces relatively steady levels of drug in the body, while the second type of pharmacotherapy should permit *ad libitum* dosing that allows the user to adjust dosing on an acute basis.[111,112] All three studies used the nicotine patch (15 mg) as one of the medications; in two studies the patch was supplemented with nicotine gum (2 mg),[113,114] and in the remaining study the patch was supplemented with nicotine nasal spray.[115] Comparison subjects receiving monotherapy were given the nicotine patch in two of these studies and nicotine gum in the third.

The results of the combination NRT meta-analysis are displayed in Table 32. The results show that the combination NRT treatment produced higher long-term abstinence rates than did NRT monotherapy. The recommendation to use combination NRT carries a strength of evidence rating of B. This is because the small number of studies in this analysis contained heterogeneous combination treatments as well as heterogeneous comparison conditions. It is important to note that the FDA has not approved a combination NRT strategy for treatment of smoking cessation. Because there is relatively little safety data on the conjoint use of NRTs, and because combination NRT could increase the risk of nicotine overdose, the panel recommends that this treatment strategy be used only with those patients unable to quit using a single type of pharmacotherapy. Combination NRT

Table 32. Meta-analysis: Efficacy of and estimated abstinence rates for combination NRT (n = 3 studies)

Factor	Number of arms	Odds ratio	Estimated abstinence rate (95% C.I.)
One NRT	3	1.0	17.4
Two NRTs	3	1.9 (1.3, 2.6)	28.6 (21.7, 35.4)

also is more expensive than is the use of a single NRT. This extra cost should be considered in making recommendations about NRT use.

Two studies have examined the impact of the combination of the nicotine patch plus nicotine gum on the suppression of the nicotine withdrawal syndrome.[111,116] These studies show that combination NRT is more effective than a single NRT.

It is unknown whether the superiority of combination therapy is due to the use of two types of delivery systems, or instead due to the fact that two delivery systems tend to produce higher blood nicotine levels than does the use of a single type of NRT. However, there is only modest evidence that using two forms of passive pharmacotherapies or increasing the dose of a single NRT increases long-term abstinence rates.[117-120] This suggests that the increment in success produced by combination NRTs may depend on the use of two distinct delivery systems: one passive and one *ad libitum*. This conclusion must remain tentative until more research is conducted on this topic. Finally, there is not yet sufficient data to determine whether combination NRTs are particularly efficacious with subpopulations of smokers (e.g., those high in nicotine dependence).

Pharmacotherapies Not Recommended by the Guideline Panel

Antidepressants Other Than Bupropion SR and Nortriptyline

Smoking is significantly more prevalent among individuals with a history of depression, and these individuals have more difficulty quitting smoking than do smokers without a history of depression.[121-123] One antidepressant, bupropion SR, has been documented as effective for smoking cessation and approved by the FDA for this use (see above). Nortriptyline also appears to be effective (see above), although the FDA has not approved this medication for treatment of tobacco dependence. Trials have investigated the use of other antidepressants for smoking cessation, including other tricyclics and selective serotonin reuptake inhibitors (SSRIs), but no published articles met selection criteria for review. Because of a paucity of data, the panel drew no conclusions about antidepressant therapy for smoking cessation except to recommend bupropion SR as a first-line agent and nortriptyline as a second-line agent.

Anxiolytics/Benzodiazepines/Beta-Blockers

A few trials have evaluated anxiolytics as a treatment for smoking cessation. Individual trials of propranolol[124] (a beta-blocker) and diazepam[125] (an anxiolytic) did not reveal a beneficial effect for these drugs compared with control interventions. Of the two studies assessing the anxiolytic buspirone that met inclusion criteria, only one revealed evidence of efficacy relative to placebo.[126,127] Because of a lack of data, no meta-analyses were conducted, and no conclusions were drawn regarding the efficacy of anxiolytics in smoking cessation.

Silver Acetate

The two randomized clinical trials[128,129] of silver acetate that met selection criteria revealed no beneficial effects for smoking cessation; therefore, the use of silver acetate as either a primary or an adjunctive treatment for smoking cessation was not supported.

Mecamylamine

Two studies meeting selection criteria evaluated the efficacy of mecamylamine for smoking cessation. In the single study that compared mecamylamine alone to placebo, no efficacy was noted.[130] In both studies, one combination of mecamylamine plus the nicotine patch was compared to placebo; in only one of these studies was the difference significant.[131] Because of these findings, the panel drew no conclusions regarding mecamylamine as a sole medication.

Pharmacotherapy for Treating Tobacco Dependence: Issues Relevant to Use

Overcoming Clinician Reluctance to Use Pharmacotherapy

Some clinicians are reluctant to recommend and prescribe pharmacotherapy for their patients who smoke. Several reasons have been cited for this reluctance, including clinician beliefs that are prevalent, but not supported by evidence. Examples of such beliefs are: smoking is a lifestyle choice and not a true dependence disorder; pharmacotherapy should be reserved for heavily dependent smokers, or used only in conjunction with an intensive cessation treatment; and smokers will be most successful if they first try to quit on their own.

Clinical and epidemiological data strongly counter these beliefs. A variety of findings show that tobacco dependence meets all accepted criteria for a drug dependence disorder. In most users, tobacco use produces tolerance, a well-characterized withdrawal syndrome, and an inability to control future use.[25] Thus, tobacco dependence warrants medical treatment just as do other drug dependence disorders and other chronic diseases.

The panel concluded that, in the vast majority of cases, it is inappropriate to reserve pharmacotherapy until patients have tried to quit on their own. Although many smokers have quit on their own, the vast majority of unaided quit attempts, between 90–95 percent, end in failure.[2,65] By using the pharmacotherapies found to be effective in this guideline, clinicians can double or triple their patients' chances of abstinence. Pharmacotherapies recommended in this guideline have been used effectively with psychosocial treatments that have varied greatly in intensity. When intensity of adjuvant treatments has been examined, data reveal that the pharmacotherapies are effective at low as well as high levels of psycho-social treatment intensity.[132,133] Therefore, clinicians should recommend effective psychosocial treatments such as counseling, in addition to pharmacotherapy, to all patients for whom it is appropriate. Finally, pharmacotherapies are effective for a broad range of smokers, not just "hardcore" smokers.

Extended Use of Pharmacotherapy

For some patients, it may be appropriate to continue pharmacotherapeutic treatment (bupropion SR or NRT) for periods longer than usually recommended. The Lung Health Study, which studied almost 4,000 smokers with early evidence COPD, reported that of the sustained quitters, 38 percent of the women and 30 percent of the men were still using nicotine gum at 12 months.[134] Other studies also have found that, among patients given free access to nicotine gum, 15-20 percent of successful abstainers continue to use the gum for a year or longer.[135,136] Although weaning should be encouraged for all smoking cessation pharmacotherapies, continued use of such medication is clearly preferable to a return to smoking with respect to health consequences. This is because, unlike smoking, these medications do not (a) contain non-nicotine toxic substances (e.g., "tar," carbon monoxide); (b) produce dramatic surges in blood nicotine levels; and/or (c) produce strong dependence.[137]

Recommending Specific Pharmacotherapy for Specific Patient Subgroups

There are five FDA-approved medications for treating tobacco dependence. Clinicians are interested in which medications to use with which patients. Unfortunately, this guideline provides little guidance on this topic because of a lack of relevant research. Some studies have directly compared the efficacies of FDA-approved pharmacotherapies;[118] however, there are too few studies to yield definitive conclusions.

More research is needed before evidence-based pharmacotherapy algorithms can be formulated; however, several factors may guide the clinician in choosing medications for specific patient subpopulations. For example, highly dependent smokers who use nicotine gum should be urged to use 4 mg, as opposed to 2 mg, gum.[109,110] Also, bupropion SR and nortriptyline have been demonstrated to be efficacious in patients trying to quit who have a history of depression.[138,139] Additionally, for patients concerned about weight gain some pharmacotherapies (e.g., bupropion SR, NRT, in particular nicotine gum) have been shown to delay but not prevent weight gain during their use. Moreover, research suggests that some treatments (e.g., NRTs) are less efficacious in women than in men.[140,141] Finally, patient preferences and patient expectations regarding outcome also are important in guiding the choice of a specific pharmacotherapy.[142] A series of clinical recommendations for pharmacotherapy selection is shown in Table 4 in Chapter 3. For a description of some of the issues related to the use of pharmacotherapy with pregnant women, please refer to the Pregnancy section in Chapter 7.

Currently, there is insufficient evidence to suggest that the use of tobacco dependence pharmacotherapies increases long-term abstinence rates among users of smokeless tobacco. Specifically, studies conducted with nicotine gum and the nicotine patch have shown that these two medications have not increased abstinence rates in this population.[143]

Use of Nicotine Replacement Therapy in Cardiovascular Patients

Soon after the nicotine patch was released, the media reported a possible link between the use of this medication and cardiovascular risk. This question has been systematically studied since that time. Separate analyses have now documented the lack of an association between the nicotine patch and acute cardiovascular events[144-146] even in patients who continued to smoke intermittently while on the nicotine patch.[147] Because of inaccurate media coverage in the past, it may be important to inform patients who are reluctant to use NRTs that there is no evidence of increased cardiovascular risk with these medications. Note that package inserts recommend caution with acute cardiovascular diseases (see Tables 33-37).

Future Research

The following pharmacotherapeutic topics require additional research:

The effectiveness of a nicotine sublingual tablet as a tobacco dependence medication.

The effectiveness of buspirone as a tobacco dependence medication.

The effectiveness of mecamylamine as a tobacco dependence medication, both used alone and in combination with other medications.

The use of sustained or long-term pharmacotherapy for treating tobacco dependence.

The use of other antidepressants or anxiolytics as tobacco dependence medications.

The relative efficacy and safety of the five FDA-approved pharmacotherapies both, in general, and for specific subpopulations (e.g., women, adolescents, smokeless users, depressed patient, post-myocardial infarction patients).

The use of combined tobacco dependence pharmacotherapies in general and for specific subpopulations (e.g., highly dependent smokers).

Table 33. Suggestions for the clinical use of bupropion SR

	Clinical use of bupropion SR (FDA approved)
Patient selection	Appropriate as a first-line pharmacotherapy for smoking cessation.
Precautions	*Pregnancy*— Pregnant smokers should be encouraged to quit first without pharmacologic treatment. Bupropion SR should be used during pregnancy only if the increased likelihood of smoking abstinence, with its potential benefits, outweighs the risk of bupropion SR treatment and potential concomitant smoking. Similar factors should be considered in lactating women. (FDA Class B) *Cardiovascular diseases*—Generally well tolerated; infrequent reports of hypertension. *Side effects*—The most common side effects reported by bupropion SR users were insomnia (35-40%) and dry mouth (10%). *Contraindications*—Bupropion SR is contraindicated in individuals with a history of seizure disorder, a history of an eating disorder, who are using another form of bupropion (Wellbutrin or Wellbutrin SR), or who have used an MAO inhibitor in the past 14 days.
Dosage	Patients should begin with a dose of 150 mg q AM for 3 days, then increase to 150 mg b.i.d. Dosing at 150 mg b.i.d. should continue for 7-12 weeks following the quit date. Unlike nicotine replacement products, patients should begin bupropion SR treatment 1-2 weeks *before* they quit smoking. For maintenance therapy, consider bupropion SR 150 mg b.i.d. for up to 6 months.
Availability	Zyban—Prescription only.
Prescribing instructions	*Cessation prior to quit date*—Recognize that some patients will lose their desire to smoke prior to their quit date, or will spontaneously reduce the amount they smoke. *Scheduling of dose*—If insomnia is marked, taking the PM dose earlier (in the afternoon, at least 8 hours after the first dose) may provide some relief. *Alcohol*—Use alcohol only in moderation.
Cost/day[a]	$3.33

[a] Cost data is based on the retail price of the medication purchased at a national chain pharmacy located in Madison, WI April 2000.

The efficacy of combining active and passive NRTs versus combining two active or two passive NRTs.

When clonidine and nortriptyline should be used in lieu of or in combination with other tobacco dependence pharmacotherapies.

The optimal combination of counseling and pharmacotherapy intensities (see Tables 38 and 39).

Table 34. Suggestions for the clinical use of nicotine gum

	Clinical use of nicotine gum (FDA approved)
Patient selection	Appropriate as a first-line pharmacotherapy for smoking cessation.
Precautions	*Pregnancy*—Pregnant smokers should be encouraged to quit first without pharmacologic treatment. Nicotine gum should be used during pregnancy only if the increased likelihood of smoking abstinence, with its potential benefits, outweighs the risk of nicotine replacement and potential concomitant smoking. Similar factors should be considered in lactating women. (FDA Class D) *Cardiovascular diseases*—NRT is not an independent risk factor for acute myocardial events. NRT should be used with caution among particular cardiovascular patient groups: those in the immediate (within 2 weeks) postmyocardial infarction period, those with serious arrhythmias, and those with serious or worsening angina pectoris. *Side effects*—Common side effects of nicotine chewing gum include mouth soreness, hiccups, dyspepsia, and jaw ache. These effects are generally mild and transient, and often can be alleviated by correcting the patient's chewing technique (see *prescribing instructions* below).
Dosage	Nicotine gum is available in 2 mg and 4 mg (per piece) doses. The 2 mg gum is recommended for patients smoking less than 25 cigarettes per day, while the 4 mg gum is recommended for patients smoking 25 or more cigarettes per day. Generally, the gum should be used for up to 12 weeks with no more than 24 pieces/day. Clinicians should tailor the dosage and duration of therapy to fit the needs of each patient.
Availability	Nicorette, Nicorette Mint—OTC only.

Table 34. Suggestions for the clinical use of nicotine gum (continued)

Prescribing instructions	*Chewing technique*—Gum should be chewed slowly until a "peppery" or "minty" taste emerges, then "parked" between cheek and gum to facilitate nicotine absorption through the oral mucosa. Gum should be slowly and intermittently "chewed and parked" for about 30 minutes or until the taste dissipates.
	Absorption—Acidic beverages (e.g., coffee, juices, soft drinks) interfere with the buccal absorption of nicotine, so eating and drinking anything except water should be avoided for 15 minutes before and during chewing.
	Scheduling of dose—Patients often do not use enough gum to get the maximum benefit: they chew too few pieces per day and they do not use the gum for a sufficient number of weeks. Instructions to chew the gum on a fixed schedule (at least one piece every 1-2 hours) for at least 1-3 months may be more beneficial than ad libitum use.
Cost/day[a]	$6.25 for 10, 2 mg pieces.
	$6.87 for 10, 4 mg pieces.

[a] Cost data is based on the retail price of the medication purchased at a national chain pharmacy located in Madison, WI April 2000.

Over-the-Counter Pharmacotherapeutic Interventions _____

Recommendation: Over-the-counter nicotine patch therapy is more efficacious than placebo and its use should be encouraged. (Strength of evidence =B)

There were three placebo-controlled studies with six arms that met selection criteria for the analysis of pharmacotherapeutic interventions in over-the-counter (OTC) settings. These three studies specifically examined the effect of patch versus placebo. The only adjuvant treatments in these studies were a self-help manual, instructions contained in the package, or written directions for using the patch. As shown in Table 40, the use of the nicotine patch in OTC settings nearly doubles abstinence rates when compared against a placebo. There were too few studies done in the OTC setting to permit meta-analysis of the OTC effect of any other pharmacotherapy.

The FDA has approved nicotine gum and the nicotine patch for OTC use. These products are identical to the patches and gum previously available only via prescription. Although the OTC status of these medications has increased their availability and use, this does not reduce the clinician's responsibility to intervene with smokers or insurers/managed care organizations to cover the costs of such treatment. Moreover, OTC availability may enhance the capacity of nonphysician clinicians to intervene comprehensively when treating tobacco dependence.

Table 35. Suggestions for the clinical use of the nicotine inhaler

	Clinical use for the nicotine inhaler (FDA approved)
Patient selection	Appropriate as a first-line pharmacotherapy for smoking cessation.
Precautions	*Pregnancy*—Pregnant smokers should be encouraged to quit first without pharmacologic treatment. The nicotine inhaler should be used during pregnancy only if the increased likelihood of smoking abstinence, with its potential benefits, outweighs the risk of nicotine replacement and potential concomitant smoking. Similar factors should be considered in lactating women. (FDA Class D)
	Cardiovascular diseases—NRT is not an independent risk factor for acute myocardial events. NRT should be used with caution among particular cardiovascular patient groups: those in the immediate (within 2 weeks) postmyocardial infarction period, those with serious arrhythmias, and those with serious or worsening angina pectoris.
	Local irritation reactions—Local irritation in the mouth and throat was observed in 40% of patients using the nicotine inhaler. Coughing (32%) and rhinitis (23%) also were common. Severity was generally rated as mild, and the frequency of such symptoms declined with continued use.
Dosage	A dose from the nicotine inhaler consists of a puff or inhalation. Each cartridge delivers 4 mg of nicotine over 80 inhalations. Recommended dosage is 6-16 cartridges/day. Recommended duration of therapy is up to 6 months. Instruct patient to taper dosage during the final 3 months of treatment.
Availability	Nicotrol Inhaler—prescription only
Prescribing instructions	*Ambient temperature*—Delivery of nicotine from the inhaler declines significantly at temperatures below 40°F. In cold weather, the inhaler and cartridges should be kept in an inside pocket or warm area.
	Duration—Use is recommended for up to 6 months with gradual reduction in frequency of use over the last 6-12 weeks of treatment.
	Absorption—Acidic beverages (e.g., coffee, juices, soft drinks) interfere with the buccal absorption of nicotine, so eating and drinking anything except water should be avoided for 15 minutes before and during inhalation.
	Best effects—Best effects are achieved by frequent puffing.
Cost/day[a]	$10.94 for 10 cartridges.

[a] Cost data is based on the retail price of the medication purchased at a national chain pharmacy located in Madison, WI April 2000.

Table 36. Suggestions for the clinical use of the nicotine nasal spray

	Clinical use for nicotine nasal spray (FDA approved)
Patient selection	Appropriate as a first-line pharmacotherapy for smoking cessation.
Precautions	*Pregnancy*—Pregnant smokers should be encouraged to quit first without pharmacologic treatment. Nicotine nasal spray should be used during pregnancy only if the increased likelihood of smoking abstinence, with its potential benefits, outweighs the risk of nicotine replacement and potential concomitant smoking. Similar factors should be considered in lactating women. (FDA Class D) *Cardiovascular diseases*—NRT is not an independent risk factor for acute myocardial events. NRT should be used with caution among particular cardiovascular patient groups: those in the immediate (within 2 weeks) postmyocardial infarction period, those with serious arrhythmias, and those with serious or worsening angina pectoris. *Nasal/airway reactions*—Some 94% of users report moderate to severe nasal irritation in the first 2 days of use; 81% still reported nasal irritation after 3 weeks, although rated severity was mild to moderate. Nasal congestion and transient changes in sense of smell and taste also were reported. Nicotine nasal spray should not be used in persons with severe reactive airway disease. *Dependency*—Nicotine nasal spray has a dependence potential intermediate between other nicotine-based therapies and cigarettes. About 15-20% of patients report using the active spray for longer periods than recommended (6-12 months), and 5% used the spray at a higher dose than recommended.
Dosage	A dose of nicotine nasal spray consists of one 0.5 mg delivery to each nostril (1 mg total). Initial dosing should be 1-2 doses per hour, increasing as needed for symptom relief. Minimum recommended treatment is 8 doses/day, with a maximum limit of 40 doses/day (5 doses/hr). Each bottle contains approximately 100 doses. Recommended duration of therapy is 3-6 months.
Availability	Nicotrol NS—Prescription only.
Prescribing instructions	*Dose delivery*—Patients should not sniff, swallow, or inhale through the nose while administering doses as this increases irritating effects. The spray is best delivered with the head tilted slightly back.
Cost/day[a]	$5.40 for 12 doses.

[a] Cost data is based on the retail price of the medication purchased at a national chain pharmacy located in Madison, WI April 2000.

Table 37. Suggestions for the clinical use of the nicotine patch

	Clinical use for the nicotine patch (FDA approved)	
Patient selection	Appropriate as a first-line pharmacotherapy for smoking cessation.	
Precautions	*Pregnancy*—Pregnant smokers should be encouraged to quit first without pharmacologic treatment. The nicotine patch should be used during pregnancy only if the increased likelihood of smoking abstinence, with its potential benefits, outweighs the risk of nicotine replacement and potential concomitant smoking. Similar factors should be considered in lactating women. (FDA Class C) *Cardiovascular diseases*—NRT is not an independent risk factor for acute myocardial events. NRT should be used with caution among particular cardiovascular patient groups: those in the immediate (within 2 weeks) postmyocardial infarction period, those with serious arrhythmias, and those with serious or worsening angina pectoris. *Skin reactions*—Up to 50% of patients using the nicotine patch will have a local skin reaction. Skin reactions are usually mild and self-limiting, but may worsen over the course of therapy. Local treatment with hydrocortisone cream (1%) or triamcinolone cream (0.5%) and rotating patch sites may ameliorate such local reactions. In less than 5% of patients, such reactions require the discontinuation of nicotine patch treatment. *Other side effects*—insomnia.	
Dosage	Treatment of 8 weeks or less has been shown to be as efficacious as longer treatment periods. 16- and 24-hour patches are of comparable efficacy. Clinicians should consider individualizing treatment based on specific patient characteristics such as previous experience with the patch, amount smoked, degree of addictiveness, etc. Finally, clinicians should consider starting treatment on a lower patch dose in patients smoking 10 or fewer cigarettes per day.	
Availability	Nicoderm CQ, Nicotrol, generic—OTC. Nicotine patches, generic (various doses)—prescription.	
Brand	Duration	Dosage
Nicoderm CQ	4 weeks then 2 weeks then 2 weeks	21 mg/24 hours 14 mg/24 hours 7 mg/24 hours
Nicotrol	8 weeks	15 mg/16 hours

Table 37. Suggestions for the clinical use of the nicotine patch (continued)

Prescribing instructions	*Location*—At the start of each day, the patient should place a new patch on a relatively hairless location, typically between the neck and waist.
	Activities—No restrictions while using the patch.
	Time—Patches should be applied as soon as the patient wakes on their quit day. With patients who experience sleep disruption, have the patient remove the 24-hour patch prior to bedtime or use the 16-hour patch.
Cost/day[a]	Brand name patches (Nicoderm CQ, Nicotrol)—$4.00-$4.50.
	Generic patches recently became available and may be less expensive.

[a] Cost data is based on the retail price of the medication purchased at a national chain pharmacy located in Madison, WI April 2000.

Table 38. Suggestions for the clinical use of clonidine

	Clinical use of clonidine **(not FDA approved for smoking cessation)**
Patient selection	Appropriate as a second-line pharmacotherapy for smoking cessation.
Precautions	*Pregnancy*—Pregnant smokers should be encouraged to quit first without pharmacologic treatment. Clonidine should be used during pregnancy only if the increased likelihood of smoking abstinence, with its potential benefits, outweighs the risk of clonidine and potential concomitant smoking and first-line pharmacotherapies have not been successful. Similar factors should be considered in lactating women. (FDA Class C)
	Side effects—Most commonly reported side effects include dry mouth (40%), drowsiness (33%), dizziness (16%), sedation (10%), and constipation (10%). As an antihypertensive medication, clonidine can be expected to lower blood pressure in most patients. Therefore, clinicians may need to monitor blood pressure when using this medication.
	Rebound hypertension—Failure to gradually reduce the dose over a period of 2-4 days may result in a rapid increase in blood pressure, agitation, confusion, and/or tremor.
Dosage	Doses used in various clinical cessation trials have varied significantly, from 0.15-0.75 mg/day PO to 0.10-0.20 mg/day transdermal (TTS), without a clear dose-response relation to cessation. Initial dosing is typically 0.10 mg b.i.d. PO or 0.10 mg/day TTS, increasing by 0.10 mg/day per week if needed. The dose duration also varied across the clinical trials, ranging from 3-10 weeks.

Table 38. Suggestions for the clinical use of clonidine (continued)

Availability	Oral: Clonidine (generic), Catapres—prescription only. Transdermal: Catapres—prescription only.
Prescribing instructions	*Initiate*—Initiate clonidine shortly before (up to 3 days), or on, the quit date. *Location (TTS Only)*—At the start of each week, the patient should place a new patch on a relatively hairless location between the neck and waist. *Activities*—Use of either form may produce sedation, a hazard while driving or operating machinery. Users should not discontinue clonidine therapy abruptly.
Cost/day[a]	Clonidine—$0.24 for 0.2 mg. Catapres (transdermal)—$3.50.

[a] Cost data is based on the retail price of the medication purchased at a national chain pharmacy located in Madison, WI April 2000.

All clinicians have specific responsibilities regarding these products, such as encouraging their use when appropriate, providing counseling and followup, encouraging total abstinence, and offering instruction on appropriate use. Additionally, patients should be urged to read the package insert and consult with their pharmacist. Finally, the clinician may advise patients regarding the selection and use of an OTC product versus a non-OTC product such as bupropion SR or a prescription nicotine replacement treatment (nasal spray or inhaler). Clinicians also may provide or recommend counseling for patients quitting with an OTC product. It should be noted that a single recent study not included within the meta-analysis reported low abstinence rates with OTC patch use.[148]

Future Research

Important topics for future research are:

The efficacy of nicotine patch and nicotine gum when access is OTC.

The extent to which individuals use pharmacotherapies optimally when access is OTC.

The extent to which the efficacy of OTC pharmacotherapy is enhanced by adjuvant treatments (e.g., pharmacist counseling, telephone counseling, computer self-help resources, clinician interventions).

The extent to which OTC status increases or reduces the use of pharmacotherapies by poor or minority populations.

Table 39. Suggestions for the clinical use of nortriptyline

	Clinical use of nortriptyline (not FDA approved for smoking cessation)
Patient selection	Appropriate as a second-line pharmacotherapy for smoking cessation.
Precautions	*Pregnancy*—Pregnant smokers should be encouraged to quit first without pharmacologic treatment. Nortriptyline should be used during pregnancy only if the increased likelihood of smoking abstinence, with its potential benefits, outweighs the risk of nortriptyline, potential concomitant smoking, and first-line pharmacotherapies have not been successful. Nortriptyline has been associated with limb reduction anomalies. *Side effects*—Most commonly reported side effects include sedation, dry mouth (64-78%), blurred vision (16%), urinary retention, lightheadedness (49%), and shaky hands (23%). *Cardiovascular effects*—Because of risk of arrhythmias, changes in contractility, and blood flow, use with extreme caution in patients with cardiovascular disease.
Dosage	Doses used in smoking cessation trials have initiated treatment at a dose of 25 mg/d, increasing gradually to a target dose of 75 –100 mg/d. Duration of treatment used in smoking cessation trials has been approximately 12 weeks.
Availability	Nortriptyline HCl (generic)—prescription only.
Prescribing instructions	Therapy is initiated 10–28 days before the quit date to allow nortriptyline to reach steady state at the target dose. *Activities*—Use may produce sedation, a hazard while driving or operating machinery. Overdose may produce marked cardiotoxic effects. Risk of overdose should be considered carefully in using nortriptyline.
Cost/day[a]	$0.74 for 75 mg.

[a] Cost data is based on the retail price of the medication purchased at a national chain pharmacy located in Madison, WI April 2000.

Table 40. Meta-analysis: Efficacy of and estimated abstinence rates for over-the-counter nicotine patch therapy (n = 3 studies)

OTC therapy	Number of arms	Estimated odds ratio (95% C.I.)	Estimated abstinence rate (95% C.I.)
Placebo	3	1.0	6.7
Over-the-counter nicotine patch therapy	3	1.8 (1.2, 2.8)	11.8 (7.5, 16.0)

7 Special Populations

Background

Many factors could potentially affect the choice, delivery, and efficacy of tobacco dependence treatments. For instance, should interventions be tailored or modified on the basis of gender, race/ethnicity, age, comorbidity, or hospitalization status? Should pregnant smokers receive pharmacotherapy? Do tobacco dependence interventions interfere with other chemical dependency treatments? These and other special issues and populations are considered in this chapter.

A variety of health care specialties can play a key role in addressing issues related to special populations (e.g., obstetricians and family practitioners for pregnant smokers; gynecologists and family practitioners for preconception counseling and general health maintenance; pediatricians, family practitioners, and dentists for children and adolescents; internists, including cardiologists, pulmonologists, oncologists, and general internists, and family practitioners for hospitalized patients; geriatricians for older smokers; and dentists and dental hygienists for smokeless tobacco users).

One over-riding issue relevant to all tobacco users considering a quit attempt is to ensure that all textual materials used (e.g., self-help brochures) are at an appropriate reading level. This is particularly important given epidemiological data showing that tobacco use rates are markedly higher among individuals of lower educational attainment.[149]

Gender

Recommendation: The same smoking cessation treatments are effective for both men and women. Therefore, except in the case of the pregnant smoker, the same interventions can be used with both men and women. (Strength of Evidence = B)

One important question regarding quitting smoking is whether men and women should receive different cessation interventions. Smoking cessation clinical trials reveal that the same treatments benefit both men and women;[140,150] however, research suggests that some treatments are less efficacious in women than in men (e.g., NRTs).[151,152]

Although research suggests that women benefit from the same interventions as do men, women may face different stressors and barriers to quitting that may be addressed in treatment. These include greater likelihood of depression, greater weight control concerns, hormonal cycles, and others.[153] This suggests that women may benefit from tobacco dependence treatments that address these topics, although few studies have examined programs targeted to one gender. Finally, women who are considering becoming pregnant may be especially receptive to tobacco dependence treatment.

Future Research _____

The following topics regarding gender require additional research:

The efficacy of interventions that are targeted to specific genders.

The impact of gender-specific motives that may increase quit attempts and success (e.g., quitting to improve fertility and reproductive health, erectile dysfunction, pregnancy outcomes, physical appearance, and osteoporosis).

Gender differences in efficacy of tobacco dependence treatments found to be effective in this guideline.

Pregnancy

Recommendation: Because of the serious risks of smoking to the pregnant smoker and the fetus, whenever possible pregnant smokers should be offered extended or augmented psychosocial interventions that exceed minimal advice to quit. (Strength of Evidence = A)

Recommendation: Although abstinence early in pregnancy will produce the greatest benefits to the fetus and expectant mother, quitting at any point in pregnancy can yield benefits. Therefore, clinicians should offer effective smoking cessation interventions to pregnant smokers at the first prenatal visit as well as throughout the course of pregnancy. (Strength of Evidence = B)

Recommendation: Pharmacotherapy should be considered when a pregnant woman is otherwise unable to quit, and when the likelihood of quitting, with its potential benefits, outweighs the risks of the pharmacotherapy and potential continued smoking. (Strength of Evidence = C)

The selection criteria for the pregnancy meta-analysis were adjusted to reflect this unique population. Abstinence data were included only if they were biochemically confirmed, due to reports of high levels of deception regarding smoking status found in pregnant women.[35-37] Studies that had followup time points of less than 5 months were included because of the desire for preparturition data. For the meta-analysis, either minimal interventions (<3 minutes) or interventions labeled as "usual care" constituted the reference condition. Seven studies met the criteria and were included in the analysis comparing augmented smoking cessation interventions with usual care in pregnant women. A "usual care" intervention with pregnant smokers typically consists of a recommendation to stop smoking, often supplemented by provision of self-help material or referral to a stop-smoking program. Extended or augmented psychosocial interventions typically involve these treatment components as well as more intensive counseling than minimal advice. As can be seen from the data in Table 41, extended or

Table 41. Meta-analysis: Efficacy of and estimated abstinence rates for augmented interventions with pregnant smokers (n = 7 studies)

Pregnant smokers	Number of arms	Estimated odds ratio (95% C.I.)	Estimated abstinence rate (95% C.I.)
Usual care	7	1.0	6.6
Augmented intervention	8	2.8 (2.2, 3.7)	16.8 (13.1, 20.5)

augmented interventions are significantly more efficacious than usual care in pregnant women.

Components of some extended or augmented psychosocial interventions are listed in Table 42. These interventions were selected from articles included in the Table 41 meta-analysis and should guide the clinician treating the pregnant smoker.

Smoking in pregnancy imparts risks to both the woman and the fetus. Cigarette smoking by pregnant women has been shown to cause adverse fetal outcomes, including stillbirths, spontaneous abortions, decreased fetal growth, premature births, low birth weight, placental abruption, sudden infant death syndrome (SIDS), cleft palates and cleft lips, and childhood cancers. Many women are motivated to quit during pregnancy, and health care professionals can take advantage of this motivation by reinforcing the knowledge that cessation will reduce health risks to the fetus and that there are postpartum benefits for both the mother and child.[157]

The first step in intervention is assessment of tobacco use status. This is especially important in a population with reported high rates of deception. Research has shown that the use of multiple choice questions (see Table 43), as opposed to a simple yes/no question can increase disclosure among pregnant women by as much as 40 percent.[158]

Quitting smoking prior to conception or early in the pregnancy is most beneficial, but health benefits result from abstinence at any time. Therefore, a pregnant smoker should receive encouragement and assistance in quitting throughout her pregnancy.

Even women who have maintained total abstinence from tobacco for 6 or more months during pregnancy have a high rate of relapse in the postpartum period.[159,160] Postpartum relapse may be decreased by continued emphasis on the relationship between maternal smoking and poor health outcomes in infants and children (SIDS, respiratory infections, asthma, and middle ear disease).[159-162] Preventing postpartum relapse is, however, an area that would benefit from future research. Table 43 outlines clinical factors to address when counseling pregnant women about smoking.

For pregnant smokers who are unable to quit with the help of an augmented intervention (see Table 42), clinicians may consider additional or alternative

Table 42. Examples of effective interventions with pregnant patients

Ershoff et al. (1989)[154]	Brief health educator discussion of risks (3-5 minutes); advised of a free smoking cessation class; and pregnancy-specific self-help materials mailed weekly for 7 weeks
Walsh et al. (1997)[155]	Physician advice regarding risks (2-3 minutes); videotape with information on risks, barriers, and tips for quitting; midwife counseling in one 10-minute session; self-help manual; and followup letters
Windsor et al. (1985)[156]	Pregnancy-specific self-help materials (*Pregnant Woman's Self-Help Guide To Quit Smoking*) and one 10-minute counseling session with a health educator
Windsor et al. (1993)[37]	Cessation skills and risk counseling in one 15-minute session by a health counselor; education on how to use pregnancy-specific self-help materials (same materials as in Windsor et al., 1985); a followup medical letter; and social support with a buddy letter, a buddy contract, and a buddy tip sheet

psychosocial treatments such as those described in Chapter 4. The exception to this would be the use of rapid smoking, which can result in extremely high blood nicotine levels.

Clinicians may choose to consider pharmacotherapy for pregnant smokers who have been unable to quit using psychosocial interventions. In such cases, the clinician and pregnant smoker must contrast the risks and unknown efficacy of pharmacotherapy in pregnant women with the substantial risks of continued smoking. Although smoking during pregnancy clearly leads to substantial risks for both the pregnant smoker and the fetus, the clinician and patient also must be aware of potential risks of different pharmacotherapies. For example, a number of studies have shown that nicotine itself presents risks to the fetus, including neurotoxicity,[163] and bupropion SR has been shown to cause seizures in 1 out of 1,000 patients.[164]

If the clinician and pregnant or lactating patient decide to use NRT pharmacotherapy, the clinician should consider monitoring blood nicotine levels to assess level of drug delivery. In addition, the clinician should consider using medication doses that are at the low end of the effective dose range, and consider choosing delivery systems that yield intermittent, rather than continuous, drug exposure (e.g., nicotine gum rather than the nicotine patch). Because none of these medications has been tested in pregnant women for efficacy in treating tobacco dependence, the relative ratio of risks to benefits is unclear. Additionally, since small amounts of these medications are passed through breast milk, they may pose some risks for nursing infants.

Table 43. Clinical practice when assisting a pregnant patient in smoking cessation

Clinical practice	Rationale
Assess pregnant woman's tobacco use status using a multiple-choice question to improve disclosure.	Many pregnant women deny smoking, and the multiple-choice question format improves disclosure. For example: Which of the following statements best describes your cigarette smoking? ■ I smoke regularly now—about the same as before finding out I was pregnant. ■ I smoke regularly now, but I've cut down since I found out I was pregnant. ■ I smoke every once in a while. ■ I have quit smoking since finding out I was pregnant. ■ I wasn't smoking around the time I found out I was pregnant, and I don't currently smoke cigarettes.
Congratulate those smokers who have quit on their own.	To encourage continued abstinence.
Motivate quit attempts by providing educational messages about the impact of smoking on both the woman's and the fetus' health.	These are associated with higher quit rates.
Give clear, strong advice to quit as soon as possible.	Quitting early in pregnancy provides the greatest benefit to the fetus.
Suggest the use of problemsolving methods and provide social support and pregnancy-specific self-help materials.	Reinforces pregnancy-specific benefits and ways to achieve cessation.
Arrange for followup assessments throughout pregnancy, including further encouragement of cessation.	The woman and her fetus will benefit even when quitting occurs late in pregnancy.
In the early postpartum period, assess for relapse and use relapse prevention strategies recognizing that patients may minimize or deny	Postpartum relapse rates are high even if a woman maintains abstinence throughout pregnancy. Relapse prevention may start during pregnancy (see Chapter 3C—Brief Strategies C1 and C2).

Future Research

The following topics regarding smoking and pregnancy require additional research:

Relapse prevention with pregnant women and women who have recently given birth.

The efficacy of relapse prevention programs for spontaneous "self-quitters."

The most efficacious amount of contact time, number of sessions, and duration for smoking cessation interventions with pregnant women.

The efficacy of various counseling and behavioral therapies and motivational interventions (e.g., physiological feedback of adverse impacts, quitting benefits).

Efficacious treatments for highly dependent smokers.

The safety and efficacy of tobacco dependence pharmacotherapy during pregnancy to the woman and the fetus, including: the relative risks and benefits of pharmacotherapy use as a function of dependence, and the appropriate formulation and timing of pharmacotherapy.

The safety and efficacy of tobacco dependence pharmacotherapy to the woman and child during nursing.

The efficacy of targeted or individualized interventions in pregnancy.

Strategies for linking preconception, pregnancy, and postpartum (including pediatric) interventions.

Racial and Ethnic Minorities

Recommendation: Smoking cessation treatments have been shown to be effective across different racial and ethnic minorities. Therefore, members of racial and ethnic minorities should be provided treatments shown to be effective in this guideline. (Strength of Evidence = A)

Recommendation: Whenever possible, tobacco dependence treatments should be modified or tailored to be appropriate for the ethnic or racial populations with which they are used. (Strength of Evidence = C)

Ethnic and racial minority groups in the United States—African Americans, American Indians/Alaska Natives, Asians and Pacific Islanders, Hispanics—experience higher mortality in a number of disease categories compared with others. For example, African Americans experience substantial excess mortality from cancer, cardiovascular disease, and infant death, all of which are directly affected by tobacco use.[165,166] American Indian/Alaska Native subgroups have some of the highest documented rates of infant mortality caused by SIDS,[167] which also is affected by tobacco use. Therefore, there is a critical need to deliver effective tobacco dependence interventions to ethnic and racial minorities. Unfortunately, there is evidence that large proportions of some racial/ethnic groups lack adequate access to primary care providers.[166] This suggests that special efforts and resources should be provided to meet the treatment needs of these populations.

There are well-documented differences between racial and ethnic minorities and whites in smoking prevalence, smoking patterns, and quitting behavior in the United States.[166,168,169] In addition, smoking prevalence and patterns vary substantially among minority subgroups.[166,167] Racial and ethnic minority groups also differ from whites in awareness of the health effects of smoking[170] and report a sense of fatalism that may affect disease prevention efforts. On the other hand, both tobacco dependence and desire to quit appear to be prevalent across all racial and ethnic groups.[166,168,169,171]

Studies have demonstrated the efficacy of a variety of smoking cessation interventions in minority populations. Nicotine patch,[172] clinician advice,[173,174] counseling,[175] tailored self-help manuals and materials, and telephone counseling[173,176] have been shown to be effective with African Americans. Nicotine patch[177] and self-help materials, including a mood management component,[178] have been shown to be effective with Hispanic smokers. Screening for tobacco use, clinician advice, clinic staff reinforcement, and followup materials have been shown to be effective for American Indian populations.[179]

Few studies have examined interventions specifically designed for particular ethnic or racial groups, and there is no consistent evidence that targeted cessation programs result in higher quit rates in these groups than do generic interventions of comparable intensity.[176] Moreover, smoking cessation interventions developed for the general population have been effective with racial and ethnic minority participants. Therefore, clinicians should offer treatments identified as effective in this guideline to their patients from all racial and ethnic groups. It is essential, however, that cessation counseling or self-help materials be conveyed in a language understood by the smoker. Additionally, culturally appropriate models or examples may increase the smoker's acceptance of treatment. Clinicians should remain sensitive to individual differences and health beliefs that may affect treatment acceptance and success in all populations (see section in Chapter 6A, Specialized Assessment).

Future Research

The following topics regarding racial and ethnic minorities require additional research:

The efficacy of targeted versus generic interventions for different racial and ethnic minority populations.

The identification of the specific barriers or impediments to treatment or treatment success (e.g., socioeconomic status, inadequate access to medical care), and the differential health effects related to smoking patterns for racial and ethnic minorities.

Motivators of cessation that are especially effective with members of racial and ethnic minorities (e.g., fear of illness requiring long-term care and disability).

Hospitalized Smokers

Recommendation: Smoking cessation treatments have been shown to be effective for hospitalized patients. Therefore, hospitalized patients should be provided smoking cessation treatments shown to be effective in this guideline. (Strength of Evidence = B)

Four studies met the selection criteria and were relevant to the analysis comparing augmented smoking cessation treatment with usual care for hospitalized patients. Because the analysis was limited to four studies, no attempt was made to categorize the augmented treatment with respect to intensity or type for the purpose of the meta-analysis. For reference only, the augmented interventions in the analyzed studies included elements such as self-help via brochure or audio/videotape, chart prompt reminding physician to advise smoking cessation, pharmacotherapy, hospital counseling, and postdischarge counseling telephone calls. As can be seen from the data in Table 44, augmented smoking cessation interventions among hospitalized patients increase rates of smoking abstinence.

It is vital that hospitalized patients attempt to quit smoking, because smoking may interfere with their recovery. Among cardiac patients, second heart attacks are more common in those who continue to smoke.[16,180] Lung, head, and neck cancer patients who are successfully treated, but who continue to smoke, are at elevated risk for a second cancer.[181-185] Additionally, smoking negatively affects bone and wound healing.[186-188]

Hospitalized patients may be particularly motivated to make a quit attempt for two reasons. First, the illness resulting in hospitalization may have been caused or exacerbated by smoking, highlighting the patient's personal vulnerability to the health risks of smoking. Second, every hospital in the United States must now be

Table 44. Meta-analysis: Efficacy of and estimated abstinence rates for augmented interventions with hospitalized smokers (n = 4 studies)

Hospitalized smokers	Number of arms	Estimated odds ratio (95% C.I.)	Estimated abstinence rate (95% C.I.)
Usual care	4	1.0	19.2
Augmented intervention	6	1.3 (1.04, 1.6)	23.3 (19.5, 27.1)

smoke free if it is to be accredited by the Joint Commission on Accreditation of Healthcare Organizations (JCAHO). As a result, every hospitalized smoker is temporarily housed in a smoke-free environment. For these reasons, clinicians should use hospitalization as an opportunity to promote smoking cessation in their patients who smoke.[189,190] Patients in long-term care facilities also should receive tobacco dependence interventions identified as efficacious in this guideline. Suggested interventions for hospitalized patients can be found in Table 45.

Future Research

The following topics regarding hospitalized patients require additional research:

The efficacy of interventions provided by different hospital personnel, including nurses.

The efficacy of pharmacotherapy with hospitalized patients.

Relapse prevention once the patient leaves the hospital.

Smokers With Psychiatric Comorbidity and/or Chemical Dependency

Recommendation: Smokers with comorbid psychiatric conditions should be provided smoking cessation treatments identified as effective in this guideline. (Strength of Evidence = C)

Recommendation: Bupropion SR and nortriptyline, efficacious treatments for smoking cessation in the general population, also are effective in treating depression. Therefore, bupropion SR and nortriptyline should be especially considered for the treatment of tobacco dependence in smokers with current or past history of depression. (Strength of Evidence = C)

Table 45. Suggested interventions for hospitalized patients

For every hospitalized patient, the following steps should be taken:

- Ask each patient on admission if he or she uses tobacco and document tobacco use status.
- For current tobacco users, list tobacco use status on the admission problem list and as a discharge diagnosis.
- Use counseling and pharmacotherapy to assist all tobacco users to maintain abstinence and to treat withdrawal symptoms.
- Provide advice and assistance on how to quit during hospitalization and remain abstinent after discharge.

Recommendation: Evidence indicates that smoking cessation interventions do not interfere with recovery from chemical dependency. Therefore, smokers receiving treatment for chemical dependency should be provided smoking cessation treatments shown to be effective in this guideline, including both counseling and pharmacotherapy. (Strength of Evidence = C)

The term "psychiatric comorbidity" refers to the co-occurrence of smoking with another psychiatric disorder. Although it is not necessary to assess for psychiatric comorbidity prior to initiating tobacco dependence treatment, psychiatric comorbidity is important to the assessment and treatment of smokers for several reasons:

Psychiatric disorders are more common among smokers than in the general population. For instance, as many as 30 percent of patients seeking smoking cessation services may have a history of depression,[121] and 20 percent or more may have a history of alcohol abuse or dependence.[191-195] Among abusers of alcohol and drugs, smoking occurs at rates well above population average (e.g., greater than 70%).[196-198] These individuals may infrequently present themselves for tobacco dependence treatment. However, such treatments could be conveniently delivered within the context of chemical dependence clinics.

Smoking cessation or nicotine withdrawal may exacerbate a patient's comorbid condition. For instance, smoking cessation may elicit or exacerbate depression among patients with a prior history of affective disorder.[199-202]

As noted in the Specialized Assessment section in Chapter 6A, smokers with psychiatric comorbidities have heightened risk for relapse to smoking after a cessation attempt.[88,191,195,202]

Although psychiatric comorbidity places smokers at increased risk for relapse, such smokers can be helped by smoking cessation treatments.[195,203-207] Currently, there is insufficient evidence to determine whether smokers with psychiatric comorbidity benefit more from specialized or tailored cessation treatments than from standard treatments.[102,208] Even though some smokers may experience exacerbation of a comorbid condition upon quitting smoking, most evidence suggests that abstinence entails little adverse impact. For instance, patients in inpatient psychiatric units are able to stop smoking with few adverse effects (e.g., little increase in aggression).[209-211] Finally, stopping smoking may affect the pharmacokinetics of certain psychiatric medications.[212] Therefore, clinicians may wish to monitor closely the actions or side effects of psychiatric medications in smokers making a quit attempt.

Evidence shows that bupropion SR is efficacious for both depression and smoking cessation. Therefore, it appears to be an appropriate medication to use with depressed smokers trying to quit. Nortriptyline is also efficacious for both depression and smoking cessation, but its side-effect profile renders it a second-line medication.

The treatment of tobacco dependence can be provided concurrent to treating patients for other chemical dependencies (alcohol and other drugs). With patients in treatment for chemical dependency, there is little evidence that patients with other chemical dependencies relapse to other drug use when they stop smoking.[209,213,214] However, such patients should be followed closely after they stop smoking.

Future Research

The following topics regarding psychiatric comorbidity and/or chemical dependency require additional research:

The relative efficacy of bupropion SR and nortriptyline versus NRT in patients with psychiatric comorbidity, including depression.

The efficacy and impact of tobacco dependence treatments within the context of other chemical dependency treatments.

The importance and efficacy of specialized assessment and tailored interventions in these populations.

Children and Adolescents

Recommendation: Clinicians should screen pediatric and adolescent patients, and their parents, for tobacco use and provide a strong message regarding the importance of totally abstaining from tobacco use. (Strength of Evidence = C)

Recommendation: Counseling and behavioral interventions shown to be effective with adults should be considered for use with children and adolescents. The content of these interventions should be modified to be developmentally appropriate. (Strength of Evidence = C)

Recommendation: When treating adolescents, clinicians may consider prescriptions for bupropion SR or NRT when there is evidence of nicotine dependence and desire to quit tobacco use. (Strength of Evidence = C)

Recommendation: Clinicians in a pediatric setting should offer smoking cessation advice and interventions to parents to limit children's exposure to second-hand smoke. (Strength of Evidence = B)

Tobacco use is a pediatric concern. In the United States, more than 6,000 children and adolescents try their first cigarette each day.[7] More than 3,000 children and adolescents become daily smokers every day,[8] resulting in approximately 1.23 million new smokers under the age of 18 each year.[7] Among adults who had ever smoked daily, 89 percent tried their first cigarette and 71 percent were daily users at or before age 18.[63] Among high school seniors who had used smokeless tobacco, 79 percent had first done so by the ninth grade.[63,215] By the time they are high school seniors, 22 percent of adolescents smoke daily.[216-218] Young people experiment with or begin regular use of tobacco for a variety of reasons related to social and parental norms, advertising, peer influence, parental smoking, weight control, and curiosity.[63,219] Nicotine dependence, however, is established rapidly even among adolescents.[220] Because of the importance of primary prevention in this population, clinicians should pay particular attention to delivering these messages to their patients. Specifically, because tobacco use often begins during preadolescence[221] clinicians should routinely assess and intervene with this population. Prevention strategies useful in more general settings can be found in the Institute of Medicine report *Growing Up Tobacco Free*.[222]

Young people vastly underestimate the addictiveness of nicotine. Of daily adolescent smokers who think that they will not smoke in 5 years, nearly 75 percent are still smoking 5–6 years later.[63] Of the nearly three-fourths of adolescents (70.2 percent) who have ever tried smoking, more than one-third (35.8 percent) became daily smokers during high school. Seventy percent of adolescent smokers wish they had never started smoking in the first place.[223] About three out of every four adolescent smokers have made at least one serious attempt to quit smoking and have failed.[224]

Tobacco Use Treatments in Children and Adolescents

A recent study has shown that adolescents' smoking status was identified in 72.4 percent of office visits, but smoking cessation counseling was provided at only 16.9 percent of clinic visits of adolescent smokers.[20] Therefore, clinicians both need to assess adolescent tobacco use and offer cessation counseling. Clinicians also should make an effort to prepare adolescents to quit smoking. For instance, clinicians may use motivational interventions such as those listed in Chapter 3B or consider techniques adapted for use with children.[56] Also, children and adolescents may benefit from community- and school-based intervention activities. The messages delivered by these programs should be reinforced by the clinician.[63]

A recent comprehensive review of adolescent cessation programs in a variety of settings has concluded that such programs produce quit rates that exceed naturally occurring quit rates, but that more and higher quality research needs to be done.[225]

Children and adolescents also benefit from the delivery to parents of information regarding second-hand smoke exposure. A review of the studies conducted by the expert panel showed that the delivery of information to parents regarding the harms of exposing children to second-hand smoke reduces childhood exposure to second-hand smoke and may reduce parental smoking rates.[162,226,227]

Because there is no evidence that bupropion SR or nicotine replacement is harmful for children and adolescents, clinicians may consider their use when tobacco dependence is obvious. However, because of the psychosocial and behavioral aspects of smoking in adolescents, clinicians should be confident of the patient's tobacco dependence and intention to quit before instituting pharmacotherapy. Factors such as degree of dependence, number of cigarettes per day, and body weight should be considered (see Table 4 for adult clinical recommendations).[228]

Future Research

The following topics regarding adolescents and children require additional research:

The efficacy of advice and counseling.

The efficacy of pharmacotherapy.

The efficacy of interventions designed specifically to motivate youth to stop using tobacco.

The efficacy of interventions designed to treat tobacco dependence in youth.

The efficacy of child-focused versus family-focused interventions.

The efficacy of treating parents' tobacco use in the context of pediatric visits.

Older Smokers

Recommendation: Smoking cessation treatments have been shown to be effective for older adults. Therefore, older smokers should be provided smoking cessation treatments shown to be effective in this guideline. (Strength of Evidence = A)

It is estimated that 13 million Americans ages 50 and older and 4.5 million adults over age 65 smoke cigarettes.[229] Smokers over the age of 65 can both quit smoking and benefit from abstinence.[16,230] Smoking cessation in older smokers can reduce the risk of myocardial infarction, death from coronary heart disease, and lung cancer. Moreover, abstinence can promote more rapid recovery from illnesses that are exacerbated by smoking and can improve cerebral circulation.[231,232] In fact, age does not appear to diminish the benefits of quitting smoking.[231]

The smoking cessation interventions that have been shown to be effective in the general population also have been shown to be effective with older smokers. Research has demonstrated the efficacy of the "4 A's" (ask, advise, assist, and arrange followup) in patients ages 50 and older.[233] Counseling interventions,[234-236] physician advice,[235] buddy support programs,[237] age-tailored self-help materials,[229,235,238] telephone counseling,[229,238] and the nicotine patch[239] have all been shown to be effective in treating tobacco use in adults ages 50 and older.

Due to particular concerns of this population (e.g., mobility issues) the use of proactive telephone counseling appears particularly promising with older smokers.

Future Research _____

The following topics regarding older smokers require additional research:

The efficacy of general tobacco use and dependence interventions, as well as those designed particularly for older smokers in promoting tobacco abstinence.

The efficacy of pharmacotherapy.

Effective methods to motivate older smokers to make a quit attempt.

8 Special Topics

Background

Many additional factors that influence the efficacy of tobacco dependence interventions were considered by the panel. These include weight gain after cessation, the treatment of tobacco users other than cigarette smokers, and institutional barriers that may interfere with tobacco users receiving treatment. This chapter provides the panel's recommendations and supporting evidence on these disparate topics.

Weight Gain After Smoking Cessation

Recommendation: The clinician should acknowledge that quitting smoking is often followed by weight gain. Additionally, the clinician should: (1) note that the health risks of weight gain are small when compared to the risks of continued smoking; (2) recommend physical activities and a healthy diet to control weight; and (3) recommend that patients concentrate primarily on smoking cessation, not weight control, until ex-smokers are confident that they will not return to smoking. (Strength of Evidence = C)

Recommendation: For smokers who are greatly concerned about weight gain, it may be most appropriate to prescribe or recommend bupropion SR or NRT, in particular nicotine gum, which have been shown to delay weight gain after quitting. (Strength of Evidence = B)

The majority of smokers who quit smoking gain weight. Most will gain fewer than 10 pounds, but there is a broad range of weight gain, with as many as 10 percent of quitters gaining as much as 30 pounds.[240-242] However, weight gain that follows smoking cessation is a negligible health threat compared with the risks of continued smoking.[242,243]

Women tend to gain slightly more weight than men do.[242] For both sexes, African Americans, people under age 55, and heavy smokers (those smoking more than 25 cigarettes/day) are at elevated risk for major weight gain.[240,242,244-248]

For some smokers, especially women, concerns about weight or fears about weight gain are motivators to start smoking or continue smoking.[249-252] Adolescents, even as young as junior high age, who are concerned about their weight initiate smoking more often than do other adolescents.[253-256]

Concern about weight varies substantially by ethnicity. For example, adolescent African American females are much less likely to report that they smoke to control weight than are European Americans.[257] This is an important area for further study, as little tobacco research focuses on women of minority ethnicities.[257]

Some evidence suggests that attempts to prevent weight gain (e.g., strict dieting) may undermine the attempt to quit smoking.[258-260] Other evidence suggests that weight gain is reduced if smoking cessation is accompanied by a moderate increase in physical activity.[261] One recent study showed that an exercise program, occurring in three 45-minute sessions per week, increases long-term smoking abstinence in women and delays weight gain when it is combined with a cognitive-behavioral smoking cessation program.[101]

Nicotine replacement—in particular, nicotine gum—appears to be effective in delaying postcessation weight gain. Moreover, there appears to be a dose-response relation between gum use and weight suppression (i.e., the greater the gum use, the less weight gain occurs). However, once nicotine gum use ceases, the quitting smoker gains an amount of weight that is about the same as if she or he had never used gum.[246,262-265]

Bupropion SR also appears to be effective in delaying post-cessation weight gain.[118,266,267] However, once bupropion SR therapy is stopped, the quitting smoker, on average, gains an amount of weight that is about the same as if she or he had not used bupropion SR.[118,266]

Postcessation weight gain appears to be caused both by increased intake (e.g., eating and alcohol consumption) and by metabolic adjustments. The involvement of metabolic mechanisms suggests that even if smokers do not increase their caloric intake upon quitting, they will, on average, gain some weight.[268-273] Once an individual relapses and begins smoking at precessation levels, he or she will usually lose some or all of the weight gained during the quit attempt.[272,274,275]

The research evidence reviewed above illustrates why concerns about weight gain are barriers to smoking abstinence. Many smokers (especially women) are concerned about their weight and fear that quitting will produce weight gain. Many also believe that they can do little to prevent postcessation weight except to return to smoking. These beliefs are especially difficult to address clinically because they are congruent with research findings; that is, the beliefs have some basis in fact.

Recommendations to Clinicians When Addressing Weight Gain

How should the clinician deal with concerns about weight gain? First, the clinician should neither deny the likelihood of weight gain nor minimize its significance to the patient. Rather, the clinician should inform the patient about the likelihood of weight gain and prepare the patient for its occurrence. However, the clinician should counter exaggerated fears about weight gain given the relatively moderate weight gain that typically occurs. Certain types of information may help prepare the patient for postcessation weight gain (see Table 46). Clinicians also should inform the patient that smoking presents a much greater health risk than the negligible health risk involved in the modest weight gain associated with smoking abstinence.

Second, before and during the quit attempt the clinician should stress that quitting smoking is the patient's primary, immediate priority, and that the patient will be most successful in the long run if he or she does not take strong measures (e.g., strict dieting) to counteract weight gain during a quit attempt (see Table 46).

Third, during the quit attempt, the clinician should offer to help the patient address weight gain (either personally or via referral) once the patient has successfully quit smoking. Specifically, the clinician should recommend that intensive weight control strategies be avoided until the patient is no longer experiencing withdrawal symptoms and is confident that he or she will not return to smoking. The patient should, however, be encouraged to maintain or adopt a healthy lifestyle, including engaging in moderate exercise, eating plenty of fruits and vegetables, and limiting alcohol consumption.[101]

Future Research

The following topics regarding weight gain during tobacco dependence treatment require additional research:

The impact of weight gain concerns on women of minority ethnicities.

Table 46. Clinician statements to help a patient prepare for, and cope with, postcessation weight gain

Clinician statements
"The great majority of smokers gain weight once they quit smoking. However, even without special attempts at dieting or exercise, weight gain is usually limited to 10 lbs."
"There is evidence that smokers will gain weight once they quit smoking, even if they do not eat more. However, there are medications that will help you quit smoking and limit or delay weight gain. I can recommend one for you."
"The amount of weight you will likely gain from quitting will be a minor health risk compared with the risks of continued smoking."
"Try to put your concerns about weight on the back burner. You are most likely to be successful if you first try to quit smoking, and then later take steps to reduce your weight. Tackle one problem at a time! After you have quit smoking successfully, we can talk about how to reduce your weight."
"I know weight is important to you, and that you don't want to gain a lot of weight. However, temporarily—just until you are confident that you have quit smoking for good—let's focus on strategies to get you healthy rather than on weight. Think about eating plenty of fruit and vegetables, getting regular exercise, getting enough sleep, and not eating a lot of fats. Right now, this is probably the best thing you can do for both your weight and your effort to quit smoking."
"Although you may gain some weight after quitting smoking, compare the importance of this with the added years of healthy living you will gain, your better appearance (less wrinkled skin, whiter teeth, fresher breath), and good feelings about quitting."

The efficacy of weight control measures during quit attempts and their effect on tobacco abstinence and weight.

The efficacy of pharmacotherapy to control weight gain during quit attempts.

The efficacy of the use of exercise to control weight gain during a quit attempt.

The impact of weight gain concerns on adolescent smoking.

Noncigarette Tobacco Products

Recommendation: Smokeless/spit tobacco users should be identified, strongly urged to quit, and treated with the same counseling cessation interventions recommended for smokers. (Strength of Evidence = B)

Recommendation: Clinicians delivering dental health services should provide brief interventions to all smokeless/spit (chewing tobacco and snuff) tobacco users. (Strength of Evidence = A)

Recommendation: Users of cigars, pipes, and other noncigarette combustible forms of tobacco should be identified, strongly urged to quit, and offered the same counseling interventions recommended for smokers. (Strength of Evidence = C)

Like cigarette smoking, the use of smokeless or spit tobacco, such as chewing tobacco and snuff, produces addiction to nicotine and has serious health consequences. Consumption of such smokeless tobacco products has increased in recent years,[276-278] especially among young males. Health risks from these products include abrasion of teeth, gingival recession, periodontal bone loss, leukoplakia, and oral cancer and cardiovascular disease.[279-281] Thus, the use of smokeless tobacco is not a safe alternative to smoking.

Cigar smoking also poses serious health risks. Cigar smokers are at higher risk for coronary heart disease, COPD, lung and other cancers, with evidence of dose-response effects.[282,283] Cigar use is particularly concerning because cigar sales in the United States also have increased nearly 50 percent between 1993 and 1997.[282] In 1997, an estimated 6 million U.S. teenagers ages 14-19 (37% of males, 16% of females) smoked at least one cigar within the past year. Clinicians also should be aware of and address the use of other noncigarette tobacco products, including pipes, cigarillos, loose tobacco, bidis, and betel quid.

A close review of the literature showed that there is evidence that dental health clinicians (e.g., dental hygienists) delivering brief advice to quit using smokeless/spit tobacco can increase abstinence rates.[284,285] Although somewhat limited, there is evidence that nonpharmacologic treatments used for smoking cessation also are effective in smokeless tobacco cessation. Therefore, clinicians should offer quitting advice and assistance to their patients who use tobacco regardless of the formulation of the tobacco product. Some information may be particularly relevant in the treatment of smokeless tobacco use. For instance, a large majority of moist snuff users have identifiable oral lesions, and this information may be useful in motivating a quit attempt.

Currently, there is insufficient evidence to suggest that the use of tobacco dependence pharmacotherapies increases long-term abstinence among users of smokeless tobacco. Specifically, studies conducted with nicotine gum and the nicotine patch have shown that these two medications have not increased abstinence rates in this population.[143]

Future Research

The following topics regarding non-cigarette tobacco products require additional research:

The efficacy of advice and counseling treatments to promote abstinence among users of noncigarette tobacco products.

The efficacy of pharmacotherapy treatments to promote abstinence among users of noncigarette tobacco products.

The efficacy of combined pharmacotherapy and counseling and behavioral therapies with users of noncigarette tobacco products.

Clinician Training

Recommendation: All clinicians and clinicians-in-training should be trained in effective strategies to assist tobacco users willing to make a quit attempt and to motivate those unwilling to quit at this time. Training appears to be more effective when coupled with systems changes. (Strength of Evidence = B)

The above recommendation is based on panel review of the published literature rather than a formal meta-analysis. Relevant studies focused primarily on physician training. Many of these studies examined the impact of training as it co-occurred with other systems changes such as reminder systems or staff education.[286,287] Training appears to be more effective when coupled with these systems changes.

Clinicians must be trained in effective tobacco use treatments if guideline recommendations are to be implemented. The importance of training is clear in that clinicians report lack of relevant knowledge as a significant barrier to intervening with their patients who use tobacco.[288-291]

Training should be directed at both clinicians-in-training as well as practicing clinicians. Training should be reinforced throughout the clinicians' education and practice.[292] For clinicians-in-training, most disciplines neither provide training, nor require competency, in tobacco use interventions. For example, an NCI expert panel found that medical schools do not consistently train students in effective smoking cessation interventions.[293] That panel recommended that a specific curriculum devoted to tobacco dependence treatment be included as part of each medical student's education. This curriculum may be taught as part of a preventive medicine or substance abuse course or as a class by itself. Similar recommendations would be relevant to virtually all other clinical disciplines. More recently, a survey of U.S. medical schools found that most medical schools (69%) did not require clinical training in tobacco dependence treatment.[289] Training in tobacco use interventions should not only transmit essential treatment skills but also inculcate the belief that cessation treatment is a standard of good practice.[294]

Practicing clinicians also would benefit from continuing education that addresses tobacco dependence treatment. This guideline recommends that clinicians be reimbursed for treating tobacco dependence and that their intervention activities be tracked. Either of these policies should foster increased interest in establishing expertise in treating tobacco use among practicing clinicians.

Several factors would promote the training of clinicians in tobacco intervention activities:[293]

Inclusion of education and training in tobacco dependence treatments in the required curricula of all clinical disciplines.

Inclusion of questions on effective tobacco dependence treatment in licensing and certification exams for all clinical disciplines.

Adoption by specialty societies of a uniform standard of competence in tobacco dependence treatment for all members.

Finally, clinicians who currently use any tobacco product should participate in treatment programs to stop their own tobacco use permanently. Clinicians have an important role as models for their patients. Therefore, it is heartening that many types of clinicians have dramatically decreased their tobacco use over the past 20 years. In a report on tobacco-use prevalence by occupation, the rate of smoking was noted to be 5.5 percent among physicians, 7.4 percent among dentists, 8.7 percent among physical therapists, and 22.0 percent among registered nurses.[295] All of these prevalence rates are lower than tobacco-use rates in the general population.

Future Research

The following topics regarding clinician training require additional research:

The efficacy of training programs for other health disciplines such as nursing, psychology, dentistry (including hygienists), social work, and pharmacy.

The effective elements in successful training programs (e.g., continuing medical education, interactive components).

The efficacy of systems changes, such as reminder systems (and performance feedback), when implemented with training programs.

Economic Aspects of Tobacco Dependence Treatments and Health Systems Interventions

Recommendation: The smoking cessation treatments shown to be efficacious in this guideline (both pharmacotherapy and counseling) are highly cost-effective relative to other reimbursed treatments (e.g., treatment of hyperlipidemia and mammography screening) and should be provided to all smokers. (Strength of Evidence = A)

Recommendation: Intensive smoking cessation interventions are especially efficacious and cost-effective, and smokers should have ready access to these services as well as to less intensive interventions. (Strength of Evidence = B)

Recommendation: Smoking cessation treatments (both pharmacotherapy and counseling) should be included as a paid or covered benefit by health benefits plans because doing so improves utilization and overall abstinence rates. (Strength of Evidence = B)

Recommendation: Sufficient resources should be allocated for clinician reimbursement and systems support to ensure the delivery of efficacious tobacco use treatments. (Strength of Evidence = C)

Recommendation: Provision of guideline-based interventions to treat tobacco use and addiction should be included in standard ratings and measures of overall health care quality (e.g., NCQA HEDIS, the Foundation for Accountability [FACCT]). (Strength of Evidence = C)

Smoking cessation treatments ranging from brief clinician advice to specialist-delivered intensive programs, including pharmacotherapy, are not only clinically effective, but also they are extremely cost-effective relative to other commonly used disease prevention interventions and medical treatments. Cost-effectiveness analyses have shown that smoking cessation treatment compares quite favorably with routinely reimbursed medical interventions such as the treatment of hypertension and hypercholesterolemia as well as preventive screening interventions such as periodic mammography or Papanicolaou smears.[28,71,75-77,296-298] Treating tobacco dependence is particularly important economically in that it can prevent a variety of costly chronic diseases, including heart disease, cancer, and pulmonary disease. In fact, smoking cessation treatment has been referred to as the "gold standard" of preventive interventions.[78]

It is important to note that smoking cessation is also cost-effective in special populations such as hospitalized patients and pregnant women. For hospitalized patients, successful tobacco abstinence not only reduces general medical costs in the short-term, but also reduces the number of future hospitalizations.[16] Smoking cessation interventions for pregnant women are especially cost-effective because they result in fewer low birth weight babies and perinatal deaths, fewer physical, cognitive, and behavioral problems during infancy and childhood, and also yield important health benefits for the mother.[299,300]

Although data suggest that, among clinical interventions, intensive interventions are more cost-effective than low-intensity interventions,[64] widely disseminated public health interventions may have even greater cost-effectiveness.[301]

The failure of a health plan to cover tobacco dependence treatment as an insured benefit could reduce access to these services and reduce the number of people seeking these services. It has been found that when smoking cessation services are provided as a fully covered benefit by a health plan in contrast to a health plan that required a significant co-pay, the overall utilization of cessation treatment increases and smoking prevalence within the health plan will decrease.[66] Moreover, the presence of prepaid or discounted prescription drug benefits increases patients' receipt of pharmacotherapy and smoking abstinence rates.[136,302,303]

Primary care clinicians frequently cite insufficient insurance reimbursement as a barrier to the provision of preventive services such as smoking cessation treatment.[304] An 8-year insurance industry study found that reimbursing physicians for provision of preventive care resulted in reported increases in exercise, seat belt use, and weight loss, as well as decreased alcohol use and a trend toward decreased smoking.[305]

It may be in the best interests of insurance companies, managed care organizations, and governmental bodies within a specific geographic area to work collectively to ensure that tobacco dependence interventions are a covered benefit. This also would allow the financial benefits of these services to be realized by all the health plans within a community.

The provision of tobacco dependence treatment should be increased by: (1) attention to health plan "report cards" (e.g., NCQA, HEDIS),[306,307] which support smoker identification and treatment; and (2) accreditation criteria used by JCAHO and other accrediting bodies that include the presence of effective tobacco assessment and intervention policies.

Future Research

The following topics regarding cost-effectiveness and health systems require additional research:

To what extent are the various tobacco dependence treatments cost-effective, both short and long term?

What is the best way to remove systemic barriers that prevent clinicians from effectively delivering tobacco dependence treatments?

What are the best systemic interventions to encourage provider and patient utilization of effective tobacco dependence treatments?

Whether reimbursement for tobacco dependence treatment is recovered later in reduced health care costs.

Evaluation of the relative costs and economic impacts of different formats of efficacious treatments (e.g., proactive telephone counseling, face-to-face contact, pharmacotherapy).

Alternative Treatment Goals: Harm Reduction

There is insufficient evidence to support a recommendation regarding harm reduction interventions. In harm reduction strategies, tobacco users alter, rather than eliminate, their use of nicotine or tobacco to reduce or avoid its harmful consequences. Many harm reduction strategies have been proposed such as reduced use of tobacco (perhaps with the conjoint use of pharmacotherapy), use of less hazardous tobacco/nicotine products, or use of less addictive tobacco/ nicotine products.[308] It is difficult to evaluate the potential benefits of harm reduction strategies because of a lack of published data. For instance, it is unknown whether public health would ultimately be better served by smokers' attempting to reduce or shift their tobacco use (e.g., smoke fewer cigarettes) rather than by making repeated quit attempts. It must be borne in mind that all types of tobacco use (e.g., smokeless, pipe, cigar) carry significant health risks. Specifically, the use of smokeless/spit tobacco is not a safe alternative to smoking. Moreover, increased health risks have been documented even in "light" smokers (less than five cigarettes per day).[309] Finally, evidence suggests that when smokers are forced to reduce their nicotine intake, they frequently engage in compensatory smoking (e.g., taking more puffs per cigarette, taking deeper puffs).[310]

In sum, it is not known whether harm reduction strategies would reduce tobacco exposure over the long-term, whether they would reduce negative health outcomes, whether their encouragement would yield greater benefits than an exclusive reliance on abstinence, and whether they might increase tobacco use prevalence by suggesting the availability of a "safe" tobacco strategy. As a result, prior to embracing any harm reduction strategy, extensive research will need to be performed on the feasibility, efficacy, and costs and benefits of these strategies. Some of the needed research includes:

Are a significant number of smokers able to maintain smoking reduction behaviors (e.g., reduced quantity) for long periods of time? What techniques promote such reductions, and what are the characteristics of those who are able to reduce and those who are unable to do so?

What degree of compensatory smoking occurs when smokers reduce the number of cigarettes smoked or smoke low tar cigarettes when:
– Aided by medications (e.g., bupropion SR or NRT)
– Unaided by medications

What are the physiologic and health impacts of smoking reduction strategies (i.e., reduced smoking rate or use of low tar and/or low nicotine cigarettes) when:
– Aided by medications (e.g., bupropion SR or NRT)
– Unaided by medications

Will a significant number of smokers use nontobacco medicines (e.g., bupropion SR and/or NRT) in lieu of smoking over the long term, and will this benefit health?

What are the public health and clinical implications of recommending a harm reduction strategy in addition to abstinence strategies (e.g., a message such as "You should quit. If you can't quit, you should try to reduce.")?

Would the forced reduction of the nicotine content of cigarettes by the tobacco companies constitute an effective societal intervention?[311]

What medications are most effective in promoting reduced smoking (short and long term) without compensatory smoking?

How effective are behavioral interventions in promoting reduced smoking (short and long term) without compensatory smoking?

References

1. Centers for Disease Control and Prevention. Perspectives in disease prevention and health promotion smoking-attributable mortality and years of potential life lost—United States, 1984. MMWR Morb Mortal Wkly Rep 1997; 46(20):444-51.

2. US Department of Health and Human Services. The health benefits of smoking cessation: A report of the Surgeon General. Atlanta (GA): US Department of Health and Human Services. Public Health Service, Centers for Disease Control, Center for Chronic Disease Prevention and Health Promotion, Office of Smoking and Health. DHHS Publication No. (CDC) 90-8416, 1990.

3. Centers for Disease Control and Prevention. Health objectives for the nation cigarette smoking among adults—United States, 1993. MMWR Morb Mortal Wkly Rep 1994;43(50):925-30.

4. Centers for Disease Control and Prevention. Cigarette smoking among adults—United States, 1995. MMWR Morb Mortal Wkly Rep 1997; 46(51):1217-20.

5. Centers for Disease Control and Prevention. Cigarette smoking among adults—United States, 1997. MMWR Morb Mortal Wkly Rep 1999;48(43):993-6.

6. Centers for Disease Control and Prevention. Tobacco use among high school students—United States, 1997. MMWR Morb Mortal Wkly Rep 1998; 47(12):229-233.

7. Centers for Disease Control and Prevention. Incidence of initiation of cigarette smoking—United States, 1965-1996. MMWR Morb Mortal Wkly Rep 1998; 47(39):837-40.

8. Gilpin E, Choi WS, Berry C, Pierce JP. How many adolescents start smoking each day in the United States? J Adolesc Health 1999;25:248-55.

9. Miller LS, Zhang X, Rice DP, Max W. State estimates of total medical expenditures attributable to cigarette smoking, 1993. Public Health Rep 1998;113(5):447-58.

10. Centers for Disease Control and Prevention. Medical care expenditures attributable to cigarette smoking—United States, 1993. MMWR 1994;43(26):469-72.

11. Thorndike AN, Rigotti NA, Stafford RS, Singer DE. National patterns in the treatment of smokers by physicians. JAMA 1998;279(8):604-8.

12. Fiore MC, Jorenby DE, Schensky AE, Smith SS, Bauer RR, Baker TB. Smoking status as the new vital sign: effect on assessment and intervention in patients who smoke. Mayo Clin Proc 1995;70(3):209-13.

13. Glynn TJ, Manley MW, Pechacek TF. Physician-initiated smoking cessation program: the National Cancer Institute trials. Prog Clin Biol Res 1990;339:11-25.

14. Jaen C, Stange K, Tumiel L, Nutting P. Missed opportunities for prevention: smoking cessation advice and the competing demands of practice. J Fam Pract 1997;45(4):348-54.

15. Russell MA, Wilson C, Taylor C, Baker CD. Effect of general practitioners' advice against smoking. BMJ 1979;2(6184):231-5.

16. Lightwood JM, Glantz SA. Short-term economic and health benefits of smoking cessation: myocardial infarction and stroke. Circulation 1997;96(4):1089-96.

17. US Department of Health and Human Services. Public Health Service. Healthy People 2000: national health promotion and disease prevention objectives. Washington (DC): US Department of Health and Human Services, Public Health Service. DHHS Publication No.(PHS) 91-50212. 1991.

18. Orleans CT. Treating nicotine dependence in medical settings: a stepped-care model. In: Orleans CT, Slade J, editors. Nicotine addiction: principles and management. New York: Oxford University Press, 1993.

19. McBride PE, Plane MB, Underbakke G, Brown RL, Solberg LI. Smoking screening and management in primary care practices. Arch Fam Med 1997;6(2):165-72.

20. Thorndike A, Ferris T, Stafford R, Rigotti N. Rates of US physicians counseling adolescents about smoking. Journal of the National Cancer Institute 1999; 91(21):1857-62.

21. Cabana M, Rand C, Powe N, Wu A, et al. Why don't physicians follow clinical practice guidelines? JAMA 1999;282(15):1458-64.

22. Jaen C, Crabtree B, Zyzanski S, Goodwin M, Stange K. Making time for smoking cessation counseling. J Fam Pract 1998;46(5):425-8.

23. Slade J. Cessation: it's time to retire the term. SRNT Newsletter 1999;5(3):1-4.

24. Jones H, Garrett B, Griffiths R. Subjective and physiological effects of intravenous nicotine and cocaine in cigarette smoking cocaine abusers. J Pharmacol Exp Ther 1999;288(1):188-97.

25. US Department of Health and Human Services. The health consequences of smoking: nicotine addiction. A report of the Surgeon General. Atlanta (GA): US Department of Health and Human Services. Public Health Service, Centers for Disease Control, Center for Chronic Disease Prevention and Health Promotion, Office of Smoking and Health. DHHS Publication No. (PHS) (CDC) 88-8406. 1988.

26. American Psychiatric Association. Practice guideline for the treatment of patients with nicotine dependence. Am J Psychiatry 1996; 153(10 (Suppl)):S1-S31.

27. American Medical Association. American Medical Association guidelines for the diagnosis and treatment of nicotine dependence: how to help patients stop smoking. Washington DC: American Medical Association, 1994.

28. British Thoracic Society. Smoking cessation guidelines and their cost-effectiveness. Thorax 1998; 53(Suppl 5, part 1):S1-S38.

29. The Cochrane Collaboration. Cochrane Database of Systematic Reviews. The Cochrane Library 1999;(4).

30. Centers for Disease Control and Prevention. Smoking cessation during previous year among adults—United States, 1990 and 1991. MMWR Morb Mortal Wkly Rep 1993;42(26):504-7.

31. Hatziandreu EJ, Pierce JP, Lefkopoulou M, Fiore MC, Mills SL, Novotny TE, et al. Quitting smoking in the United States in 1986. J Natl Cancer Inst 1990; 82(17):1402-6.

32. Fiore MC, Baker TB. Smoking cessation treatment and the good doctor club [editorial]. Am J Public Health 1995;85(2):161-3.

33. Mezzich J, Kraemer H, Worthington D, Coffman G. Assessment of agreement among several raters formulating multiple diagnoses. J Psychiatr Res 1981;16:29-39.

34. Fleiss J. Statistical methods for rates and proportions. New York: Wiley, 1981.

35. Kendrick JS, Zahniser SC, Miller N, Salas N, Stine J, Gargiullo PM, et al. Integrating smoking cessation into routine public prenatal care: the Smoking Cessation in Pregnancy project. Am J Public Health 1995;85(2):217-22.

36. Walsh RA, Redman S, Adamson L. The accuracy of self-report of smoking status in pregnant women. Addict Behav 1996;21(5):675-9.

37. Windsor RA, Lowe JB, Perkins LL, Smith-Yoder D, Artz L, Crawford M, et al. Health education for pregnant smokers: its behavioral impact and cost benefit. Am J Public Health 1993;83(2):201-6.

38. DerSimonian R, Laird N. Meta-analysis in clinical trials. Control Clin Trials 1986; 7(3):177-88.

39. Hosmer DW, Lemeshow S. Applied logistic regression. New York: Wiley, 1989.

40. Eddy DM. FAST*PRO software for meta-analysis by the confidence profile method [manual for software]. San Diego (CA): Academic Press, 1992.

41. Centers for Disease Control and Prevention. Physician and other health care professional counseling of smokers to quit—United States, 1991. MMWR Morb Mortal Wkly Rep 1993;42(44):854-7.

42. Hayward RA, Meetz HK, Shapiro MF, Freeman HE. Utilization of dental services: 1986 patterns and trends. J Public Health Dent 1989;49(3):147-52.

43. Tomar SL, Husten CG, Manley MW. Do dentists and physicians advise tobacco users to quit? J Am Dent Assoc 1996;127(2):259-65.

44. National Cancer Institute. Tobacco and the clinician: interventions for medical and dental practice. Monogr Natl Cancer Inst 5, 1-22. NIH Publication No. 94-3693. 1994.

45. Ockene JK. Smoking intervention: The expanding role of the physician. Am J Public Health 1987;77(7):782-3.

46. Pederson LL, Baskerville JC, Wanklin JM. Multivariate statistical models for predicting change in smoking behavior following physician advice to quit smoking. Prev Med 1982;11(5):536-49.

47. Woller SC, Smith SS, Piasecki TM, Jorenby DE, Helberg CP, Love RR, et al. Are clinicians intervening with their patients who smoke? A "real-world" assessment of 45 clinics in the upper Midwest. WMJ 1995;94(5):266-72.

48. Goldstein MG, Niaura R, Willey-Lessne C, DePue J, Eaton C, Rakowski W, et al. Physicians counseling smokers. A population-based survey of patients' perceptions of health care provider-delivered smoking cessation interventions. Arch Intern Med 1997;157(12):1313-9.

49. Stange K, Zyzanski S, Jaen C, et al. Illuminating the black box: a description of 4454 patient visits of 138 family physicians. J Fam Pract 1998;46(5):377-89.

50. Gilchrist V, Miller RS, Gillanders WR, Scheid DC, Logue EE, Iverson DC, et al. Does family practice at residency teaching sites reflect community practice? J Fam Pract 1993;37(6):555-63.

51. Lichtenstein E, Hollis J. Patient referral to a smoking cessation program: who follows through? J Fam Pract 1992;34(6):739-44.

52. Glynn TJ, Manley MW. How to help your patients stop smoking: a National Cancer Institute manual for physicians. Bethesda, MD: NIH Publication No. 89-3064. 1989.

53. Kottke TE, Solberg LI, Brekke ML. Beyond efficacy testing: introducing preventive cardiology into primary care. Am J Prev Med 1990;6(2 Suppl):77-83.

54. Mecklenburg RE, Christen AG, Gerbert B, Gift MC. How to help your patients stop using tobacco: a National Cancer Institute manual for the oral health team 1990. US DHHS Public Health Service, National Institutes of Health, National Cancer Institute. NIH Publication No. 91-3191, 1991.

55. Rundmo T, Smedslund G, Gotestam KG. Motivation for smoking cessation among the Norwegian public. Addict Behav 1997;22(3):377-86.

56. Colby SM, Barnett NP, Monti PM, Rohsenow DJ, et al. Brief motivational interviewing in a hospital setting for adolescent smoking: a preliminary study. J Consult Clin Psychol 1998;66(3):574-8.

57. Miller W, Rolnick S. Motivational interviewing: preparing people to change addictive behavior. New York: Guilford, 1991.

58. Prochaska J, Goldstein MG. Process of smoking cessation. Implications for clinicians. Clin Chest Med 1991;12(4):727-35.

59. Westman EC, Behm FM, Simel DL, Rose JE. Smoking behavior on the first day of a quit attempt predicts long-term abstinence. Arch Intern Med 1997;157(3):335-40.

60. Zhu SH, Stretch V, Balabanis M, Rosbrook B, Sadler G, Pierce JP. Telephone counseling for smoking cessation: effects of single-session and multiple-session interventions. J Consult Clin Psychol 1996;64(1):202-11.

61. Brandon TH, Tiffany ST, Obremski K, Baker TB. Postcessation cigarette use: the process of relapse. Addict Behav 1990;15:105-14.

62. Carroll KM. Relapse prevention as a psychosocial treatment: A review of controlled clinical trials. Exp Clin Psychopharmacol 1996;4(1):46-54.

63. US Department of Health and Human Services. Preventing tobacco use among young people. A report of the Surgeon General. Atlanta (GA): US Department of Health and Human Services, Public Health Service, Centers for Disease Control and Prevention, National Center for Chronic Disease Prevention and Health Promotion, Office on Smoking and Health. 1994.

64. Cromwell J, Bartosch WJ, Fiore MC, Hasselblad V, Baker T. Cost-effectiveness of the clinical practice recommendations in the AHCPR Guideline for Smoking Cessation. Agency for Health Care Policy and Research. JAMA 1997; 278(21):1759-66.

65. Fiore MC, Novotny TE, Pierce JP, Giovino GA, Hatziandreu EJ, Newcomb PA, et al. Methods used to quit smoking in the United States. Do cessation programs help? [published erratum appears in JAMA 1991 Jan 16;265(3):358]. JAMA 1990; 263(20):2760-5.

66. Curry SJ, Grothaus LC, McAfee T, Pabiniak C. Use and cost effectiveness of smoking-cessation services under four insurance plans in a health maintenance organization. N Engl J Med 1998;339(10):673-9.

67. Aakko E, Piasecki TM, Remington P, Fiore MC. Smoking cessation services offered by health insurance plans for Wisconsin State Employees. WMJ 1999;98:14-8.

68. Group Health Association of America. HMO industry profile: 1993 edition. Washington DC: Group Health Association of America, 1993.

69. Barker D, Orleans CT, Schauffler H. Tobacco treatment services should be covered under Medicaid (letter). Tob Control 1998; 7(1):92.

70. McPhillips-Tangum C. Results from the first annual survey on Addressing Tobacco in Managed Care. Tob Control 1998;7(Suppl):S11-S14.

71. Cummings SR, Rubin SM, Oster G. The cost-effectiveness of counseling smokers to quit. JAMA 1989;261(1):75-9.

72. Tengs T, Adams M, Pliskin J, Safran D, Seigel J, Weinstein M, et al. Five-hundred life-saving interventions and their cost effectiveness. Risk Anal 1995;15(3):369-90.

73. US Department of Health and Human Services. Healthy People 2000: National health promotion and disease prevention objectives. Washington DC: US Department of Health and Human Service, Public Health Service, 1995.

74. US Department of Health and Human Services. Healthy People 2010 (Conference Edition, in Two Volumes). Washington DC. 2000.

75. Eddy DM. The economics of cancer prevention and detection: getting more for less. Cancer 1981;47(5 Suppl):1200-9.

76. Eddy DM. Setting priorities for cancer control programs. J Natl Cancer Inst 1986; 76(2):187-199.

77. Oster G, Huse DM, Delea TE, Colditz GA. Cost-effectiveness of nicotine gum as an adjunct to physician's advice against cigarette smoking. JAMA 1986; 256(10):1315-8.

78. Eddy DM. David Eddy ranks the tests. Harv Health Lett 1992;11.

79. Jackson SE, Cheneweth D, Glover ED, Holbert D, White D. Study indicates smoking cessation improves workplace absenteeism rate. Occup Health Saf 1989; 58(13):13, 15-6, 18.

80. Kristein M. How much can business expect to profit from smoking cessation? Prev Med 1993;12(2):358-81.

81. Ahluwalia JS. Reaching the medically underserved with the AHCPR guideline. Tob Control 1997; 6(Suppl 1):S29-S32.

82. Ahluwalia J, Gibson C, Kenney R, Wallace D, Resnicow K. Smoking status as a vital sign. J Gen Intern Med 1999;14(7):402-8.

83. Chang HC, Zimmerman LH, Beck JM. Impact of chart reminders on smoking cessation practices of pulmonary physicians. Am J Respir Crit Care Med 1995; 152(3):984-7.

84. Robinson MD, Laurent SL, Little JM, Jr. Including smoking status as a new vital sign: it works! J Fam Pract 1995;40(6):556-61.

85. Yarnall KS, Rimer BK, Hynes D, Watson G, Lyna PR, Woods-Powell CT, et al. Computerized prompts for cancer screening in a community health center. J Am Board Fam Pract 1998;11(2):96-104.

86. Dijkstra A, de Vries H, Roijackers J, van Breukelen G. Tailored interventions to communicate stage-matched information to smokers in different motivational stages. J Consult Clin Psychol 1998;66(3):549-57.

87. Velicer W, Prochaska JO, Fava J, Laforge R, Rossi JS. Interactive versus noninteractive interventions and dose-response relationships for stage-matched smoking cessation programs in a managed care setting. Health Psychol 1999; 18(1):21-8.

88. Gilbert D, Crauthers D, Mooney D, McClernon F, Jensen R. Effects of monetary contingencies on smoking relapse: influences of trait depression, personality, and habitual nicotine intake. Exp Clin Psychopharmacol 1999;7(2):174-81.

89. Jaen CR, Stange KC, Nutting PA. Competing demands of primary care: a model for the delivery of clinical preventive services. J Fam Pract 1994;38(2):166-71.

90. Killen JD, Fortmann SP, Davis L, Varady A. Nicotine patch and self-help video for cigarette smoking cessation. J Consult Clin Psychol 1997;65(4):663-72.

91. Killen JD, Fortmann SP, Kraemer HC, Varady AN, Davis L, Newman B. Interactive effects of depression symptoms, nicotine dependence, and weight change on late smoking relapse. J Consult Clin Psychol 1996;64(5):1060-7.

92. Shiffman S, Paty JA, Gnys M, Kassel JA, Hickcox M. First lapses to smoking: within-subjects analysis of real-time reports. J Consult Clin Psychol 1996; 64(2):366-79.

93. Fiore MC. The new vital sign. Assessing and documenting smoking status. JAMA 1991;266(22):3183-3184.

94. Pallonen UE, Velicer WF, Prochaska JO, Rossi JS, Bellis JM, Tsoh JY, et al. Computer-based smoking cessation interventions in adolescents: description, feasibility, and six-month follow-up findings. Substance Use & Misuse 1998; 33(4):935-65.

95. Strecher VJ, Kreuter M, Den Boer DJ, Kobrin S, Hospers HJ, Skinner CS. The effects of computer-tailored smoking cessation messages in family practice settings. J Fam Pract 1994;39(3):262-70.

96. Davis AL, Faust R, Ordentlich M. Self-help smoking cessation and maintenance programs: a comparative study with 12-month follow-up by the American Lung Association. Am J Public Health 1984;74(11):1212-7.

97. Lando HA, Rolnick S, Klevan D, Roski J, Cherney L, Lauger G. Telephone support as an adjunct to transdermal nicotine in smoking cessation. Am J Public Health 1997;87(10):1670-4.

98. Ossip-Klein DJ, Giovino GA, Megahed N, Black PM, Emont SL, Stiggins J, et al. Effects of a smoker's hotline: results of a 10-county self-help trial. J Consult Clin Psychol 1991;59(2):325-32.

99. Platt S, Tannahill A, Watson J, Fraser E. Effectiveness of antismoking telephone helpline: follow up survey. BMJ 1997;314(7091):1371-5.

100. Kenford SL, Fiore MC, Jorenby DE, Smith SS, Wetter D, Baker TB. Predicting smoking cessation. Who will quit with and without the nicotine patch. JAMA 1994;271(8):589-94.

101. Marcus B, Albrecht A, King T, Parisi Aea. Efficacy of exercise as an aid for smoking cessation in women. Arch Intern Med 1999;159:1229-34.

102. Hall SM, Munoz RF, Reus VI. Cognitive-behavioral intervention increase abstinence rates for depressive-history smokers. J Consult Clin Psychol 1994; 62(1):141-6.

103. Hall SM, Munoz RF, Reus VI, Sees KL, Duncan C, Humfleet GL, et al. Mood management and nicotine gum in smoking treatment: a therapeutic contact and placebo-controlled study. J Consult Clin Psychol 1996;64(5):1003-9.

104. Abbot N, Stead L, White ABJ, Ernst E. Hypnotherapy for smoking cessation (Cochrane Review). The Cochrane Library 1999;(1).

105. Dijkstra A, de Vries H, Roijackers J, van Breukelen G. Tailoring information to enhance quitting in smokers with low motivation to quit: three basic efficacy questions. Health Psychol 1998;17(6):513-9.

106. Strecher V. Computer-tailored smoking cessation materials: a review and discussion. Patient Education and Counseling 1999;36:107-17.

107. Velicer W, Prochaska JO. An expert system intervention for smoking cessation. Patient Education and Counseling 1999;36:119-29.

108. Cinciripini PM, Lapitsky L, Seay S, Wallfisch A, Kitchens K, Van V. The effects of smoking schedules on cessation outcome: can we improve on common methods of gradual and abrupt nicotine withdrawal? J Consult Clin Psychol 1995; 63(3):388-99.

109. Herrera N, Franco R, Herrera L, Partidas A, Rolando R, Fagerstrom KO. Nicotine gum, 2 and 4 mg, for nicotine dependence. A double-blind placebo-controlled trial within a behavior modification support program. Chest 1995; 108(2):447-51.

110. Kornitzer M, Kittel F, Dramaix M, Bourdoux P. A double blind study of 2 mg versus 4 mg nicotine-gum in an industrial setting. J Psychosom Res 1987;31(2):171-6.

111. Fagerstrom KO. Combined use of nicotine replacement products. Health Values 1994;18(3):15-20.

112. Stapleton J. Commentary: Progress on nicotine replacement therapy for smokers [comment]. BMJ 1999; 318(7179):289.

113. Kornitzer M, Bousten M, Thijs J, Gustavsson G. Efficiency and safety of combined use of nicotine patches and nicotine gum in smoking cessation: A placebo controlled double-blind trial. Eur Respri J 1993;6(17 Suppl):630s.

114. Puska P, Korhonen H, Vartiainen E, Urjanheimo EL, Gustavsson G, Westin A. Combined use of nicotine patch and gum compared with gum alone in smoking cessation: a clinical trial in North Karelia. Tob Control 1995;4:231-5.

115. Blondal T, Gudmundsson LJ, Olafsdottir I, Gustavsson G, Westin A. Nicotine nasal spray with nicotine patch for smoking cessation: Randomized trial with six year follow up. BMJ 1999;318:285-8.

116. Fagerstrom KO. Effectiveness of nicotine patch and nicotine gum as individual versus combined treatments for tobacco withdrawal symptoms. Psychopharmacology 1993;111:271-7.

117. Hughes JR, Cummings KM, Hyland A. Ability of smokers to reduce their smoking and its association with future smoking cessation. Addiction 1999;94(1):109-14.

118. Jorenby DE, Leischow S, Nides M, Rennard S, Johnston JA, Hughes AR, et al. A controlled trial of sustained-release bupropion, a nicotine patch, or both for smoking cessation. N Engl J Med 1999;340(9):685-91.

119. Jorenby DE, Smith SS, Fiore MC, Hurt RD, Offord KP, Croghan IT, et al. Varying nicotine patch dose and type of smoking cessation counseling. JAMA 1995; 274(17):1347-52.

120. Tonnesen P, Paoletti P, Gustavsson G, Russell MA, Saracci R, Gulsvik A, et al. Higher dosage nicotine patches increase one-year smoking cessation rates: results from the European CEASE trial. Eur Respir J 1999;13:238-246.

121. Anda RF, Williamson DF, Escobedo LG, Mast EE, Giovino GA, Remington PL. Depression and the dynamics of smoking. A national perspective. JAMA 1990; 264(12):1541-5.

122. Breslau N, Kilbey MM, Andreski P. Nicotine withdrawal symptoms and psychiatric disorders: findings from an epidemiologic study of young adults. Am J Psychiatry 1992;149(4):464-9.

123. Glassman AH, Helzer JE, Covey LS, Cottler LB, Stetner F, Tipp JE, et al. Smoking, smoking cessation, and major depression. JAMA 1990;264(12):1546-9.

124. Farebrother MJB, Pearce SJ, Turner P, Appleton DR. Propranolol and giving up smoking. Br J Dis Chest 1980;74(1):95-96.

125. Wei H, Young D. Effect of clonidine on cigarette cessation and in the alleviation of withdrawal symptoms. Br J Addict 1988;83:1221-6.

126. Cinciripini PM, Lapitsky L, Seay S, Wallfisch A, Meyer WJ 3rd, van Vunakis H. A placebo-controlled evaluation of the effects of buspirone on smoking cessation: differences between high- and low-anxiety smokers [published erratum appears in J Clin Psychopharmacol 1995 Dec;15(6):408]. J Clin Psychopharmacol 1995; 15(3):182-91.

127. Schneider NG, Olmstead RE, Steinberg C, Sloan K, Daims RM, Brown HV. Efficacy of buspirone in smoking cessation: a placebo-controlled trial. Clin Pharmacol Ther 1996;60(5):568-75.

128. Hymowitz N, Eckholdt H. Effects of a 2.5-mg silver acetate lozenge on initial and long-term smoking cessation. Prev Med 1996;25(5):537-46.

129. Jensen EJ, Schmidt E, Pedersen B, Dahl R. The effect of nicotine, silver acetate, and placebo chewing gum on the cessation of smoking. The influence of smoking type and nicotine dependence. Int J Addict 1991;26(11):1231-3.

130. Rose JE, Behm FM, Westman EC. Nicotine-mecamylamine treatment for smoking cessation: the role of pre-cessation therapy. Exp Clin Psychopharmacol 1998; 6(3):331-43.

131. Rose JE, Behm FM, Westman EC, Levin ED, Stein RM, Ripka GV. Mecamylamine combined with nicotine skin patch facilitates smoking cessation beyond nicotine patch treatment alone. Clin Pharmacol Ther 1994;56:86-99.

132. Fiore MC, Kenford SL, Jorenby DE, Wetter DW, Smith SS, Baker TB. Two studies of the clinical effectiveness of the nicotine patch with different counseling treatments. Chest 1994;105(2):524-33.

133. Silagy C, Mant D, Fowler G, Lodge M. The effectiveness of nicotine replacement therapies in smoking cessation. Online J Curr Clin Trials 1994; Doc No 113:[7906 words; 110 paragraphs].

134. Nides MA, Rakos RF, Gonzales D, Murray RP, Tashkin DP, Bjornson B, et al. Predictors of initial smoking cessation and relapse through the first 2 years of the Lung Health Study. J Consult Clin Psychol 1995;63(1):60-9.

135. Hajek P, Jackson P, Belcher M. Long-term use of nicotine chewing gum. Occurrence, determinants, and effect on weight gain. JAMA 1988;260(11):1593-6.

136. Hughes JR, Wadland WC, Fenwick JW, Lewis J, Bickel WK. Effect of cost on the self-administration and efficacy of nicotine gum: A preliminary study. Prev Med 1991;20:486-96.

137. Henningfield JE. Nicotine medications for smoking cessation. [Review] [101 refs]. N Engl J Med 1995;333(18):1196-203.

138. Hall SM, Reus VI, Munoz RF, Sees KL, Humfleet G, Hartz DT, et al. Nortriptyline and cognitive-behavioral therapy in the treatment of cigarette smoking. Arch Gen Psychiatry 1998;55(8):683-90.

139. Hayford K, Patten C, Rummans D, Offord KP, et al. Efficacy of buproprion for smoking cessation in smokers with a former history of major depression or alcoholism. Br J Psychiatry 1999;174:173-8.

140. Bjornson W, Rand C, Connett JE, Lindgren P, Nides M, Pope F, et al. Gender differences in smoking cessation after 3 years in the Lung Health Study. Am J Public Health 1995;85(2):223-30.

141. Gritz ER, Thompson B, Emmons K, Ockene JK, McLerran DF, Nielsen IR. Gender differences among smokers and quitters in the Working Well Trial. Prev Med 1998; 27(4):553-61.

142. Hughes J, Goldstein MG. Recent advances in the pharmacotherapy of smoking. JAMA 1999;281(1):72-6.

143. Hatsukami D, Severson H. Oral spit tobacco: addiction, prevention, and treatment. Nicotine Tob Res 1999;1:21-44.

144. Benowitz NL, Gourlay SG. Cardiovascular toxicity of nicotine: implications for nicotine replacement therapy. J Am Coll Cardiol 1997;29(7):1422-31.

145. Joseph AM, Norman SM, Ferry LH, Prochazka AV, Westman EC, Steele BG, et al. The safety of transdermal nicotine as an aid to smoking cessation in patients with cardiac disease. N Engl J Med 1996;335(24):1792-8.

146. Mahmarian JJ, Moye LA, Nasser GA, et al. Nicotine patch therapy in smoking cessation reduces the extent of exercise-induced myocardial ischemia. J Am Coll Cardiol 1997;30(1):125-30.

147. Working Group for the Study of Transdermal Nicotine in Patients with Coronary Artery Disease. Nicotine replacement therapy for patients with coronary artery disease. Arch Intern Med 1994;154:989-95.

148. Leischow S, Muramoto ML, Cook G, Merikle E, Castellini S, Otte PS. OTC nicotine patches: effectiveness alone and with brief physician intervention. Am J Health Behav 1999;23(1):61-9.

149. Pierce J, Giovino G, Hatziandreu E, Shopland D. National age and sex differences in quitting smoking. J Psychoactive Drugs 1989;21(3):293-8.

150. Gritz E, Thompson B, Emmons K, Ockene J, McLerran DF, Nielsen IR. Gender differences among smokers and quitter in the working well trial. Prev Med 1998; 27:553-61.

151. Perkins KA. Sex differences in nicotine versus nonnicotine reinforcement as determinants of tobacco smoking. Exp Clin Psychopharmacol 1996;4(2):166-77.

152. Wetter D, Fiore MC, Jorenby D, Kenford S, Smith S, Baker T. Gender differences in smoking. J Consult Clin Psychol 1999;67(4):555-62.

153. Gritz ER, Nielsen IR, Brooks LA. Smoking cessation and gender: the influence of physiological, psychological, and behavioral factors. [Review] [86 refs]. J Am Med Womens Assoc 1996;51(1-2):35-42.

154. Ershoff DH, Mullen PD, Quinn VP. A randomized trial of a serialized self-help smoking cessation program for pregnant women in an HMO. Am J Public Health 1989;79(2):182-7.

155. Walsh RA, Redman S, Brinsmead MW, Byrne JM, Melmeth A. A smoking cessation program at a public antenatal clinic. Am J Public Health 1997; 87(7):1201-4.

156. Windsor RA, Cutter G, Morris J, Reese Y, Manzella B, Bartlett EE, et al. The effectiveness of smoking cessation methods for smokers in public health maternity clinics: a randomized trial. Am J Public Health 1985;75(12):1389-92.

157. Wisborg K, Henriksen TB, Obel C, Skajaa E. Smoking during pregnancy and hospitalization of the child. Pediatrics 1999;104(4):e46 (internet).

158. Mullen PD, Carbonari JP, Tabak ER, Glenday MC. Improving disclosure of smoking by pregnant women. Am J Obstet Gynecol 1991;165(2):409-13.

159. Edwards N, Sims-Jones N. Smoking and smoking relapse during pregnancy and postpartum: results of a qualitative study. Birth 1998;25(2):94-100.

160. Ko M, Schulken ED. Factors related to smoking cessation and relapse among pregnant smokers. Am J Health Behav 1998;22(2):83-9.

161. McBride CM, Pirie PL. Postpartum smoking relapse. Addict Behav 1990; 15(2):165-8.

162. Severson HH, Andrews JA, Lichtenstein E, Wall M, Akers L. Reducing maternal smoking and relapse: long-term evaluation of a pediatric intervention. Prev Med 1997;26(1):120-30.

163. Slotkin TA. Fetal nicotine or cocaine exposure: which one is worse? J Pharmacol Exp Ther 1998;285(3):931-45.

164. Dunner D, Zisook S, Billow A, Batey S, et al. A prospective safety surveillance study for bupropion sustained-release in the treatment of depression. J Clin Psychiatry 1998;59(7):366-73.

165. Centers for Disease Control. Cigarette smoking among blacks and other minority populations. MMWR Morb Mortal Wkly Rep 1987;36(25):405-7.

166. US Department of Health and Human Services. African Americans and tobacco. Surgeon General's Report on African Americans and Tobacco. 1998.

167. Coultas DB, Gong H, Jr., Grad R, Handler A, McCurdy SA, Player R, et al. Respiratory diseases in minorities of the United States. Am J Respir Crit Care Med 1994;149(3 Pt 2):S93-S131.

168. Orleans CT, Schoenbach VJ, Salmon MA, Strecher VJ, Kalsbeek W, Quade D, et al. A survey of smoking and quitting patterns among Black Americans. Am J Public Health 1989;79(2):176-81.

169. Stotts RC, Glynn TJ, Baquet CR. Smoking cessation among blacks. J Health Care Poor Underserved 1991;2(2).

170. Brownson RC, Jackson-Thompson J, Wilkerson JC, Davis JR, Owens NW, Fisher EB, Jr. Demographic and socioeconomic differences in beliefs about the health effects of smoking. Am J Public Health 1992;82(1):99-103.

171. Royce JM, Hymowitz N, Corbett K, Hartwell TD, and Orlandi MA, for the COMMIT Research Group. Smoking cessation factors among African Americans and whites. Am J Public Health 1993;83(2):220-6.

172. Ahluwalia JS, McNagny SE, Clark WS. Smoking cessation among inner-city African Americans using the nicotine transdermal patch. J Gen Intern Med 1998; 13(1):1-8.

173. Lipkus IM, Lyna PR, Rimer BK. Using tailored interventions to enhance smoking cessation among African-Americans as a community health center. Nicotine Tob Res 1999;1:77-85.

174. Royce JM, Ashford A, Resnicow K, Freeman HP, Caesar AA, Orlandi MA. Physician- and nurse-assisted smoking cessation in Harlem. J Natl Med Assoc 1995;87(4):291-9.

175. Schorling J, Roach J, Baturka N, et al. A trial of church-based smoking cessation interventions for rural African Americans. Prev Med 1997;26(1):92-101.

176. Orleans CT, Boyd NR, Bingler R, Sutton C, Fairclough D, Heller D, et al. A self-help intervention for African American smokers: tailoring cancer information service counseling for a special population. Prev Med 1998;27(5 Pt 2):S61-S70.

177. Leischow SJ, Hill A, Cook G. The effects of transdermal nicotine for the treatment of Hispanic smokers. Am J Health Behav 1996;20(5):304-11.

178. Munoz RF, Marin BV, Posner SF, Perez-Stable EJ. Mood management mail intervention increases abstinence rates for Spanish-speaking Latino smokers. Am J Community Psychol 1997;25(3):325-43.

179. Johnson KM, Lando HA, Schmid LS, Solberg LI. The GAINS project: outcome of smoking cessation strategies in four urban Native American clinics. Giving American Indians No-smoking Strategies. Addict Behav 1997;22(2):207-18.

180. Multiple Risk Factor Intervention Trial Research Group. Multiple Risk Factor Intervention Trial. Risk factor changes and mortality results. JAMA 1982; 248(12):1465-77.

181. Browman GP, Wong G, Hodson I, Sathya J, Russell R, McAlpine L, et al. Influence of cigarette smoking on the efficacy of radiation therapy in head and neck cancer. N Engl J Med 1993;328(3):159-63.

182. Fujisawa T, Lizasa T, et al. Smoking before surgery predicts poor long-term survival in patients with stage I non-small-cell lung carcinomas. J Clin Oncol 1999; 17(7):2086-91.

183. Gritz E. Smoking and smoking cessation in cancer patients. British Journal of Addict 1991;86:549-54.

184. Kawahara M, Ushijima S, et al. Second primary tumours in more than 2-year disease-free survivors of small-cell lung cancer in Japan: the role of smoking cessation. Br J Cancer 1998;78(3):409-12.

185. Richardson G, Tucker M, Venzon D. Smoking cessation after successful treatment of small-cell lung cancer is associated with fewer smoking-related second primary cancers. Ann Intern Med 1993;119(5):383-90.

186. Chang L, Buncke G, et al. Cigarette smoking, plastic surgery, and microsurgery. J Reconstr Microsurg 1996;12(7):467-74.

187. Grossi SG, Genco RJ, Machtei EE, et al. Assessment of risk for periodontal diseases. II. Risk indicators for alveolar bone loss. J Periodontol 1995;66:23-9.

188. Jones RM. Smoking before surgery: the case for stopping [editorial]. BMJ (Clin Res Ed) 1985;290(6484):1763-4.

189. Hurt RD, Lauger GG, Offord KP, Bruce BK, Dale LC, McClain FL, et al. An integrated approach to the treatment of nicotine dependence in a medical center setting: Description of the initial experience. J Gen Intern Med 1992;7:114-6.

190. Stevens VJ, Glasgow RE, Hollis JF, Lichtenstein E, Vogt TM. A smoking-cessation intervention for hospital patients. Med Care 1993; 31(1):65-72.

191. Brandon TH. Negative affect as motivation to smoke. Curr Psychol Res Rev 1994; 3(33):33-7.

192. Breslau N. Psychiatric co-morbidity of smoking and nicotine dependence. Behav Genet 1995;25:95-101.

193. Breslau N, Kilbey MM, Andreski P. DSM-III-R nicotine dependence in young adults: prevalence, correlates and associated psychiatric disorders. Addiction 1994;89(6):743-54.

194. Glassman AH, Stetner F, Walsh BT, Raizman PS, Fleiss JL, Cooper TB, et al. Heavy smokers, smoking cessation, and clonidine: results of a double-blind, randomized trial. JAMA 1988;259(19):2863-6.

195. Hall SM, Munoz RF, Reus VI, Sees KL. Nicotine, negative affect, and depression. J Consult Clin Psychol 1993;61(5):761-7.

196. Budney AJ, Higgins ST, Hughes JR, Bickel WK. Nicotine and caffeine use in cocaine-dependent individuals. J Subst Abuse 1993;5(2):117-30.

197. Clemmey P, Brooner R, Chutuape MA, Kidorf M, Stitzer M. Smoking habits and attitudes in a methadone maintenance treatment population. Drug Alcohol Depend 1997;44(2-3):123-32.

198. DiFranza JR, Guerrera MP. Alcoholism and smoking. J Stud Alcohol 1990; 51(2):130-5.

199. Covey LS, Glassman AH, Stetner F. Cigarette smoking and major depression. [Review] [28 refs]. J Addict Dis 1998;17(1):35-46.

200. Ginsberg JP, Klesges RC, Johnson KC, Eck LH, Meyers AW, Winders SA. The relationship between a history of depression and adherence to a multicomponent smoking-cessation program. Addict Behav 1997;22(6):783-7.

201. Glassman AH. Cigarette smoking: implications for psychiatric illness. Am J Psychiatry 1993;150(4):546-53.

202. Glassman AH, Covey LS, Dalack GW, Stetner F, Rivelli SK, Fleiss J, et al. Smoking cessation, clonidine, and vulnerability to nicotine among dependent smokers. Clin Pharmacol Ther 1993;54(6):670-9.

203. Breckenridge JS. Smoking by outpatients. Hosp Community Psychiatry 1990; 41(4):454-5.

204. Burling TA, Marshall GD, Seidner AL. Smoking cessation for substance abuse inpatients. J Subst Abuse 1991;3(3):269-76.

205. Hartman N, Jarvik ME, Wilkins JN. Reduction of cigarette smoking by use of a nicotine patch [letter]. Arch Gen Psychiatry 1989;46(3):289.

206. Hartman N, Leong GB, Glynn SM, Wilkins JN, Jarvik ME. Transdermal nicotine and smoking behavior in psychiatric patients. Am J Psychiatry 1991;148(3):374-5.

207. Ziedonis DM, George TP. Schizophrenia and nicotine use: report of a pilot smoking cessation program and review of neurobiological and clinical issues. Schizophr Bull 1997;23(2):247-54.

208. Zelman DC, Brandon TH, Jorenby DE, Baker TB. Measures of affect and nicotine dependence predict differential response to smoking cessation treatments. J Consult Clin Psychol 1992;60(6):943-52.

209. Hurt RD, Eberman KM, Slade J, Karan L. Treating nicotine addiction in patients with other addictive disorders. In: Orleans CT, Slade J, editors. Nicotine addiction: principles and management. New York: Oxford, 1993:310-326.

210. Resnick MP. Treating nicotine addiction in patients with psychiatric comorbidity. In: Orleans CT, Slade J, editors. New York: Oxford University Press, 1993: 327-36.

211. Smith C, Pristach C, Cartagena M. Obligatory cessation of smoking by psychiatric inpatients. Psychiatr Serv 1999;50(1):91-4.

212. Hughes JR. Pharmacotherapy for smoking cessation: unvalidated assumptions, anomalies, and suggestions for future research. [Review]. J Consult Clin Psychol 1993;61(5):751-60.

213. Bobo JK, McIlvain HE, Lando HA, Walker RD, Leed-Kelly A. Effect of smoking cessation counseling on recovery from alcoholism: findings from a randomized community intervention trial. Addiction 1998;93(6):877-87.

214. Ellingstad T, Sobell L, Sobell M, Cleland P. Alcohol abusers who want to quit smoking: implications for clinical treatment. Drug Alcohol Depend 1999; 54(3):259-65.

215. UMI News and Information Services. Drug use by America's young people. MTFP 1998.

216. Green DE. Teenage smoking: immediate and long-term patterns. Washington DC: National Institute of Education, 1979.

217. Johnston L, O'Malley PM, Bachman JG. National survey results on drug use from monitoring the future study. 1975-1994: vol. 1, secondary school students. Bethesda, Maryland: US Department of Health and Human Services, Public Health Service, National Institutes of Health, National Institute on Drug Abuse. NIH Publication No. 95-4025. 1995.

218. Pierce JP, Gilpin E. How long will today's new adolescent smoker be addicted to cigarettes? Am J Public Health 1996;86(2):253-6.

219. Pierce JP, Choi WS, Gilpin E, Farkas AJ, et al. Tobacco industry promotion of cigarettes and adolescent smoking. JAMA 1998;279(7):511-5.

220. Centers for Disease Control and Prevention. Trends in smoking initiation among adolescents and young adults: United States, 1980-89. MMWR Morb Mortal Wkly Rep 1995;44(28):521-5.

221. DiFranza, JR. Preventing teenage tobacco addiction. J Fam Pract 1992;34(6):753-6.

222. Lynch B, Bonnie RJ, editors. Institute of Medicine Committee on Preventing Nicotine Addiction in Children and Youths. Growing up tobacco free: preventing nicotine addiction in children and youths. Washington (DC): Natl Acad Press, 1994.

223. Centers for Disease Control and Prevention. Fastats. Fastats: CDC Publication 1999; www.cdc.gov/nchswww/fastats/smoking.htm.

224. Moss AJ, Allen KF, Giovino GA, Mills SL. Recent trends in adolescent smoking, smoking-uptake correlates, and expectations about the future. Adv Data 1992; (221):1-28.

225. Sussman S, Lichtman K, Ritt A, Pallonen UE. Effects of thirty-four adolescent tobacco use cessation and prevention trials on regular users of tobacco products. Substance Use & Misuse 1999;34(11):1469-503.

226. Wahlgren DR, Hovell MF, Slymen DJ, Conway TL, Hofstetter CR, Jones JA. Predictors of tobacco use initiation in adolescents: a two-year prospective study and theoretical discussion. Tob Control 1997;6(2):95-103.

227. Wall MA, Severson HH, Andrews JA, Lichtenstein E, Zoref L. Pediatric office-based smoking intervention: impact on maternal smoking and relapse. Pediatrics 1995;96(4 Pt 1):622-8.

228. Smith TA, House RFJ, Croghan IT, Gauvin TR, Colligan RC, Offord KP, et al. Nicotine patch therapy in adolescent smokers. Pediatrics 1996;98(4 (Pt 1)):659-67.

229. Rimer BK, Orleans CT, Fleisher L, Cristinzio S, Resch N, Telepchak J, et al. Does tailoring matter? The impact of a tailored guide on ratings and short-term smoking-related outcomes for older smokers. Health Educ Res 1994;9(1):69-84.

230. Cohen D, Fowlie S. Changing lifelong habits of elderly people. BMJ 1992; 304:1055-6.

231. Hermanson B, Omenn GS, Kronmal RA, Gersh BJ. Beneficial six-year outcome of smoking cessation in older men and women with coronary artery disease. Results from the CASS registry. N Engl J Med 1988;319(21):1365-9.

232. Rogers RL, Meyer JS, Judd BW, et al. Abstention from cigarette smoking improves cerebral perfusion among elderly chronic smokers. JAMA 1985;253(20):2970-4.

233. Boyd NR. Smoking cessation: a four-step plan to help older patients quit. [Review] [21 refs]. Geriatrics 1996;51(11):52-7.

234. Burton LC, Paglia MJ, German PS, Shapiro S, Damiano AM, The Medicare Preventive Services Research Team. The effect among older persons of a general preventive visit on three health behaviors: smoking, excessive alcohol drinking, and sedentary lifestyle. Prev Med 1995;24(5):492-7.

235. Morgan GD, Noll EL, Orleans CT, Rimer BK, Amfoh K, Bonney G. Reaching midlife and older smokers: tailored interventions for routine medical care. Prev Med 1996;25(3):346-54.

236. Vetter NJ, Ford D. Smoking prevention among people aged 60 and over: a randomized controlled trial. Age Ageing 1990;19(3):164-8.

237. Kviz FJ, Clark MA, Crittenden KS, Freels S, Warnecke RB. Age and readiness to quit smoking. Prev Med 1994;23(2):211-22.

238. Ossip-Klein DJ, Carosella AM, Krusch DA. Self-help interventions for older smokers. Tob Control 1997;6(3):188-93.

239. Orleans CT, Resch N, Noll E, Keintz MK, Rimer BK, Brown TV, et al. Use of transdermal nicotine in a state-level prescription plan for the elderly. A first look at 'real-world' patch users. JAMA 1994;271(8):601-7.

240. Froom P, Melamed S, Benbassat J. Smoking cessation and weight gain. [Review] [61 refs]. J Fam Pract 1998;46(6):460-4.

241. Klesges RC, Winders SE, Meyers AW, Eck LH, Ward KD, Hultquist CM, et al. How much weight gain occurs following smoking cessation? A comparison of weight gain using both continuous and point prevalence abstinence. J Consult Clin Psychol 1997;65(2):286-91.

242. Williamson DF, Madans J, Anda RF, Kleinman JC, Giovino GA, Byers T. Smoking cessation and severity of weight gain in a national cohort. N Engl J Med 1991;324(11):739-45.

243. Burnette MM, Meilahn E, Wing RR, Kuller LH. Smoking cessation, weight gain, and changes in cardiovascular risk factors during menopause: the Healthy Women Study. Am J Public Health 1998;88(1):93-6.

244. Becona E, Vazquez FL. Smoking cessation and weight gain in smokers participating in a behavioral treatment at 3-year follow-up. Psychol Rep 1998; 82(3 Pt 1):999-1005.

245. Caan B, Coates A, Schaefer C, Finkler L, Sternfeld B, Corbett K. Women gain weight 1 year after smoking cessation while dietary intake temporarily increases. J Am Diet Assoc 1996;96(11):1150-5.

246. Emont SC, Cummings KM. Weight gain following smoking cessation: a possible role for nicotine replacement in weight management. Addict Behav 1987;12:151-5.

247. Frederick SL, Hall SM, Humfleet GL, Munoz RF. Sex differences in the relation of mood to weight gain after quitting smoking. Exp Clin Psychopharmacol 1996; 4(2):178-85.

248. Klesges RC, Ward KD, Ray JW, Cutter G, Jacobs DRJ, Wagenknecht LE. The prospective relationships between smoking and weight in a young, biracial cohort: the Coronary Artery Risk Development in Young Adults Study. J Consult Clin Psychol 1998;66(6):987-93.

249. Gritz ER, Crane LA. Use of diet pills and amphetamines to lose weight among smoking and nonsmoking high school seniors. Health Psychol 1991;10(5):330-5.

250. Gritz ER, Klesges RC, Meyers AW. The smoking and body weight relationship: implications for intervention and postcessation weight control. Ann Behav Med 1989;11(4):144-53.

251. Klesges RC, Klesges LM. Cigarette smoking as a dietary strategy in a university population. Int J Eat Disord 1988;7:413-19.

252. Klesges RC, Meyers AW, Klesges LM, La Vasque ME. Smoking, body weight, and their effects on smoking behavior: A comprehensive review of the literature. Psychol Bull 1989; 106(2):204-30.

253. French S, Perry C, Leon G, Fulkerson J. Weight concerns, dieting behavior, and smoking initiation among adolescents: a prospective study. Am J Public Health 1994;84(11):1818-20.

254. Gritz E, Crane LA. Use of diet pills and amphetamines to lose weight among smoking and nonsmoking high school seniors. Health Psychol 1991;10(5):330-5.

255. Klesges RC, Elliott VE, Robinson LA. Chronic dieting and the belief that smoking controls body weight in a biracial, population-based adolescent sample. Tob Control 1997;6(2):89-94.

256. Tomeo C, Field A, Berkey C, et al. Weight concerns, weight control behavior, and smoking initiation. Pediatrics 1999;104(4):918-24.

257. Camp D, Klesges RC, Relyea G. The relationship between body weight concerns and adolescent smoking. Health Psychol 1993;12(1):24-32.

258. Hall SM, Tunstall CD, Vila KL, Duffy J. Weight gain prevention and smoking cessation: Cautionary findings. Am J Public Health 1992;82(6):799-803.

259. Perkins KA. Issues in the prevention of weight gain after smoking cessation. Ann Behav Med 1994;16:46-52.

260. Pirie PL, McBride CM, Hellerstedt W, Jeffery RW, Hatsukami D, Allen S, et al. Smoking cessation in women concerned about weight. Am J Public Health 1992; 82(9):1238-43.

261. Kawachi I, Troisi RJ, Rotnitzky AG, Coakley EH. Can physical activity minimize weight gain in women after smoking cessation? Am J Public Health 1996; 86(7):999-1004.

262. Dale LC, Schroeder DR, Wolter TD, Croghan IT, Hurt RD, Offord KP. Weight change after smoking cessation using variable doses of transdermal nicotine replacement. J Gen Intern Med 1998;13(1):9-15.

263. Doherty K, Militello FS, Kinnunen T, Garvey AJ. Nicotine gum dose and weight gain after smoking cessation. J Consult Clin Psychol 1996;64(4):799-807.

264. Gross J, Stitzer ML, Maldonado J. Nicotine replacement: effects on postcessation weight gain. J Consult Clin Psychol 1989;57(1):87-92.

265. Nides M, Rand C, Dolce J, Murray R, O'Hara P, Voelker H et al. Weight gain as a function of smoking cessation and 2-mg nicotine gum use among middle-aged smokers with mild lung impairment in the first 2 years of the Lung Health Study. Health Psychol 1994;13(4):354-61.

266. Hurt RD, Sachs DP, Glover ED, Offord KP, Johnston JA, Dale LC, et al. A comparison of sustained-release bupropion and placebo for smoking cessation. N Engl J Med 1997;337(17):1195-202.

267. Jorenby DE. New developments in approaches to smoking cessation. [Review] [33 refs]. Curr Opin Pulm Med 1998;4(2):103-6.

268. Gray CL, Cinciripini PM, Cinciripini LG. The relationship of gender, diet patterns, and body type to weight change following smoking reduction: a multivariate approach. J Subst Abuse 1995;7(4):405-23.

269. Hatsukami D, LaBounty L, Hughes J, Laine D. Effects of tobacco abstinence on food intake among cigarette smokers. Health Psychol 1993;12(6):499-502.

270. Hofstetter A, Schutz Y, Jequier E, Wahren J. Increased 24-hour energy expenditure in cigarette smokers. N Engl J Med 1986;314(2):79-82.

271. Klesges LM, Shumaker SA, editors. Proceedings of the national working conference on smoking and body weight. Health Psychol 1992;11(suppl):1-22.

272. Moffatt RJ, Owens SG. Cessation from cigarette smoking: changes in body weight, body composition, resting metabolism, and energy consumption. Metabolism 1991;40(5):465-70.

273. Schwid SR, Hirvonen MD, Keesey RE. Nicotine effects on body weight: a regulatory perspective. Am J Clin Nutr 1992;55(4):878-884.

274. Noppa H, Bengtsson C. Obesity in relation to smoking: a population study of women in Goteborg, Sweden. Prev Med 1980;9(4):534-43.

275. Stamford BA, Matter S, Fell RD, Papanek P. Effects of smoking cessation on weight gain, metabolic rate, caloric consumption, and blood lipids. Am J Clin Nutr 1986; 43(4):486-94.

276. Glover ED, Glover PN. Smokeless tobacco cessation and nicotine reduction therapy. In: Smoking and tobacco control: monograph 2 Smokeless tobacco or health: An international perspective U S Department of Health and Human Services, Public Health Service, National Institutes of Health, NIH Publication No 92-3461 1992;291-296.

277. Marcus AC, Crane LA, Shopland DR, Lynn WR. Use of smokeless tobacco in the United States: recent estimates from the current population survey. NCI Monogr 1989;(8):17-23.

278. Maxwell, J. The Maxwell consumer report: the smokeless tobacco industry in 1994. Richmond, VA, The Wheat First Butcher Singer. 1995.

279. Bolinder G, Alfredsson L, Englund A, et al. Smokeless tobacco use and increased cardiovascular mortality among Swedish construction workers. Am J Public Health 1994;84:399-404.

280. Glover ED, Schroeder KL, Henningfield JE, Severson HH, Christen AG. An interpretative review of smokeless tobacco research in the United States: Part I. J Drug Educ 1988;18(4):285-310.

281. Krall E, Garvey A, et al. Alveolar bone loss and tooth loss in male cigar and pipe smokers. J Am Dent Assoc 1999;130:57-64.

282. Iribarren C, Tekawa I, Sidney S, Friedman G. Effect of cigar smoking on the risk of cardiovascular disease, chronic obstructive pulmonary disease, and cancer in men. JAMA 1999;340(23):1773-80.

283. National Cancer Institute. Cigars: Health effects and trends. Smoking and Tobacco Control Monograph No.9. Bethesda, Maryland, National Cancer Institute. NIH Publication No. 98-4302. 1998.

284. Severson HH, Andrews JA, Lichtenstein E, Gordon JS, Barckley MF. Using the hygiene visit to deliver a tobacco cessation program: results of a randomized clinical trial. J Am Dent Assoc 1998;129(7):993-9.

285. Stevens VJ, Severson H, Lichtenstein E, Little SJ, Leben J. Making the most of a teachable moment: a smokeless-tobacco cessation intervention in the dental office. Am J Public Health 1995;85(2):231-5.

286. Lancaster, T., Silagy, C., Fowler, G., and Spiers, I. Training health professionals in smoking cessation. Cochrane Database of Systematic Reviews. Issue 4. 1999.

287. Ockene J, Zapka J. Changing provider behaviour: provider education and training. Tob Control 1997;6(Suppl 1):S63-S67.

288. Cummings KM, Giovino G, Sciandra R, Koenigsberg M, Emont SL. Physician advice to quit smoking: who gets it and who doesn't. Am J Prev Med 1987; 3(2):69-75.

289. Ferry LH, Grissino L, Runfola P. Tobacco dependence curricula in US undergraduate medical education. JAMA 1999;282(9):825-829.

290. Scott CS, Neighbor WE. Preventive care attitudes of medical students. Soc Sci Med 1985;1(3):299-305.

291. Wechsler H, Levine S, Idelson RK, Rohman M, Taylor JO. The physician's role in health promotion- a survey of primary-care practitioners. Massachusetts Department of Public Health 1983;308(2):97-100.

292. Jones C. Response to a smoking cessation workshop by family practice resident physicians. Tob Control 1993;2:30-4.

293. Fiore MC, Epps RP, Manley MW. A missed opportunity. Teaching medical students to help their patients successfully quit smoking. JAMA 1994; 271(8):624-6.

294. Kottke TE, Solberg LI, Brekke ML, Conn SA, Maxwell P, Brekke MJ. A controlled trial to integrate smoking cessation advice into primary care practice: Doctors helping smokers, round III. J Fam Pract 1992;34(6):701-8.

295. Nelson DE, Emont SL, Brackbill RM, Cameron LL, Peddicord J, Fiore MC. Cigarette smoking prevalence by occupation in the United States. A comparison between 1978 to 1980 and 1987 to 1990. J Occup Med 1994;36(5):516-25.

296. Croghan IT, Offord KP, Evans RW, Schmidt S, Gomez-Dahl LC, Schroeder DR, et al. Cost-effectiveness of treating nicotine dependence: the Mayo Clinic experience. Mayo Clin Proc 1997;72(10):917-24.

297. Meenan RT, Stevens VJ, Hornbrook MC, La Chance PA, Glasgow RE, Hollis, et al. Cost-effectiveness of a hospital-based smoking cessation intervention. Med Care 1998;36(5):670-8.

298. Plans-Rubio P. Cost-effectiveness of cardiovascular prevention programs in Spain. Int J Technol Assess Health Care 1998;14(2):320-9.

299. Lightwood JM, Phibbs C, Glantz SA. Short-term health and economic benefits of smoking cessation: low birth weight. Pediatrics 1999;104(6):1312-20.

300. Marks JS, Koplan JP, Hogue CJ, Dalmat ME. A cost-benefit/cost-effectiveness analysis of smoking cessation for pregnant women. Am J Prev Med 1990; 6(5):282-9.

301. Warner KE. Cost effectiveness of smoking-cessation therapies. Interpretation of the evidence and implications for coverage. [Review] [41 refs]. PharmacoEconomics 1997;11(6):538-49.

302. Cox JL, McKenna JP. Nicotine gum: does providing it free in a smoking cessation program alter success rates? J Fam Pract 1990;31(3):278-80.

303. Johnson RE, Hollis JF, Stevens VJ, Woodson GT. Patterns of nicotine gum use in a health maintenance organization. DICP 1991;25(7-8):730-5.

304. Henry RC, Ogle KS, Snellman LA. Preventive medicine: Physician practices, beliefs, and perceived barriers for implementation. Fam Med 1987;19(2):110-3.

305. Logsdon DN, Lazaro CM, Meier RV. The feasibility of behavioral risk reduction in primary medical care. Am J Prev Med 1989;5(5):249-56.

306. Centers for Disease Control and Prevention. Use of clinical preventive services by adults aged <65 years enrolled in health-maintenance organizations—United States, 1996. MMWR Morb Mortal Wkly Rep 1998;47(29):613-9.

307. Davis RM. Healthcare report cards and tobacco measures. Tob Control 1997; 6(Suppl 1):570-7.

308. Hughes JR. Applying harm reduction to smoking. Tob Control 1995; 4(Suppl 2):S33-S38.

309. Rosengren A, Wilhelmsen L, Wedel H. Coronary heart-disease, cancer, and mortality in male middle-aged light smokers. J Intern Med 1992;231(4):357-62.

310. US Department of Health and Human Services. The FTC cigarette test method for determining tar, nicotine, and carbon monoxide yields of US cigarettes: report of the NCI expert committee. Bethesda, MD, National Institutes of Health Publication. Publication No. 96-4028. 1996.

311. Henningfield J, Benowitz N, Slade J, Houston T, Davis RM, Deitchman S. Reducing the addictiveness of cigarettes. Tob Control 1998;7:281-93.

Glossary

Abstinence percentage. The percentage of smokers who achieve long-term abstinence from smoking. The most frequently used abstinence measure for this guideline was the percentage of smokers in a group or treatment condition who were abstinent at a followup point that occurred at least 5 months after treatment.

Acupuncture. A treatment involving the placement of needles in specific areas of the body with the intent to promote abstinence from tobacco use.

All-comers. Individuals included in a tobacco treatment study regardless of whether they sought to participate. For example, if treatment was delivered to all smokers visiting a primary care clinic, the treatment population would be coded as "all-comers." Presumably, individuals who seek to participate in tobacco treatment studies ("want-to-quit" smokers) are likely more motivated to quit, and studies limited to these individuals may produce higher quit rates. All-comers can be contrasted with "want-to-quit" populations.

Anxiolytic. A medication used to reduce anxiety symptoms.

Aversive smoking. Several types of therapeutic techniques that involve smoking in an unpleasant or concentrated manner. These techniques pair smoking with negative associations or responses. Notable examples include rapid smoking, rapid puffing, focused smoking, and satiation smoking.

Biochemical confirmation. The use of biological samples (expired air, blood, saliva, or urine) to measure tobacco-related compounds such as thiocyanate, cotinine, nicotine, and carboxyhemoglobin to verify users' reports of abstinence.

Bupropion SR (bupropion sustained-release). A non-nicotine aid to smoking cessation originally developed and marketed as an antidepressant. It is chemically unrelated to tricyclics, tetracyclics, selective serotonin re-uptake inhibitors, or other known antidepressant medications. Its mechanism of action is presumed to be mediated through its capacity to block the re-uptake of dopamine and norepinephrine centrally.

Cigarette fading/smoking reduction prequit. An intervention strategy designed to reduce the number of cigarettes smoked or nicotine intake prior to a patient's quit date. This may be accomplished through advice to cut down or by systematically restricting access to cigarettes. This category includes interventions using computers and/or strategies to accomplish prequitting reductions in cigarette consumption or nicotine intake.

Clinician. A professional directly providing health care services.

Clinic screening system. The strategies used in clinics and practices for the delivery of clinical services. Clinic screening system interventions involve changes in protocols designed to enhance the identification of and intervention with patients who smoke. Examples include affixing tobacco use status stickers to patients' charts, expanding the vital signs to include tobacco use, and incorporating tobacco-use status items into patient questionnaires.

Clonidine. An alpha-2-adrenergic agonist typically used as an antihypertensive medication, but also documented in this guideline as an effective medication for smoking cessation. The U.S. Food and Drug Administration (FDA) has not approved clonidine as a smoking cessation aid.

Compensatory smoking. When a smoker inhales more smoke, or smokes more intensely, to compensate for reductions in nicotine content of tobacco smoke, or number of cigarettes smoked/day.

Contingency contracting/instrumental contingencies. Interventions where individuals earn rewards for cigarette abstinence and/or incur costs or unpleasant consequences for smoking. To receive this classification code, actual, tangible consequences had to be contingent on smoking or abstinence. Thus, simple agreements about a quit date, or other agreements between treatment providers and patients without specifiable consequences, were not included in this category. Deposits refunded based on study attendance and/or other incentives that are not contingent on smoking abstinence or relapse did not receive this code.

Continuous abstinence. A measure of tobacco abstinence based on whether subjects are continuously abstinent from smoking/tobacco use from their quit day to a designated outcome point (e.g., end of treatment, 6 months after the quit day).

Cue exposure/extinction. Interventions that repeatedly expose patients to smoking-related cues in the absence of nicotine reinforcement in an attempt to extinguish affective/motivational responding to such cues. This includes treatments where patients are encouraged to perform the smoking self-administration ritual, excepting inhalation.

Diazepam. A benzodiazepine anxiolytic; medication intended to reduce anxiety.

Environmental tobacco smoke (ETS). Also known as "second-hand smoke." The smoke inhaled by an individual not actively engaged in smoking but due to exposure to ambient tobacco smoke.

Exercise/fitness component. Refers to an intervention that contains a component related to exercise/fitness. The intensity of interventions falling within this category varied from the mere provision of information/advice about exercise/fitness to exercise classes.

Extra-treatment social support component. Interventions or elements of an intervention wherein patients are provided with tools or assistance in obtaining social support outside of treatment. This category is distinct from intra-treatment social support, in which social support is delivered directly by treatment staff.

Foundation for Accountability (FACCT). A consumer- and purchaser-driven organization that develops patient-oriented measures of health care quality.

First-line pharmacotherapy for tobacco dependence. First-line pharmacotherapies have been found to be safe and effective for tobacco dependence treatment and have been approved by the FDA for this use. First-line medications have established empirical record of efficacy, and should be considered first as part of tobacco dependence treatment except in cases of contraindications.

Formats. Refers to a smoking cessation intervention delivery strategy. This includes self-help, proactive telephone counseling, individual counseling, and group counseling.

Health Plan Employer Data and Information Set (HEDIS). Serves as a "report card" for providing information on quality, utilization, enrollee access and satisfaction, and finances for managed care organizations and other health care delivery entities.

Higher intensity counseling. Refers to interventions that involve extended contact between clinicians and patients. It was coded based on the length of contact between clinicians and patients (greater than 10 minutes). If that information was unavailable, it was coded based on the content of the contact between clinicians and patients.

Hotline/helpline. See Telephone hotline/helpline.

Hypnosis. Also hypnotherapy. A treatment by which a clinician attempts to induce an altered attention state and heightened suggestibility in a tobacco user for the purpose of promoting abstinence from tobacco use.

Intent-to-treat analysis. Treatment outcome analyses where abstinence percentages are based on all subjects randomized to treatment conditions, rather than on just those subjects who completed the intervention or those who could be contacted at followup.

Intra-treatment social support. Refers to an intervention component that is intended to provide encouragement, a sense of concern, and interested empathic listening as part of the treatment.

Joint Commission on Accreditation of Healthcare Organizations (JCAHO). An independent, not-for-profit organization that evaluates and accredits more than 19,500 health care organizations in the United States, including hospitals, health care networks, managed care organizations, and health care organizations that provide home care, long-term care, behavioral health care, laboratory, and ambulatory care services.

Logistic regression. Statistical technique to determine the statistical association or relation between/among two or more variables, and where one of the variables, the dependent variable, is dichotomous (has only two levels of magnitude) (e.g., abstinent vs. smoking).

Low-intensity counseling. Low-intensity counseling refers to interventions that involve contact between clinicians and patients and that last between 3 and 10 minutes. If the information on length of contact was unavailable, it was coded based on the description of content of the clinical intervention.

Managed care organizations (MCOs). Any group implementing health care using managed care concepts, including preauthorization of treatment, utilization review, and a fixed network of providers.

Meta-analysis. A statistical technique that estimates the impact of a treatment or variable across a set of related studies, publications, or investigations.

Minimal counseling. Minimal counseling refers to interventions that involve very brief contact between clinicians and patients. It was coded based on the length of contact between clinicians and patients (3 minutes or less). If that information was unavailable, it was coded based on the content of the clinical intervention.

Motivation. A type of intervention designed to bolster patients' resolve to quit through manipulations such as setting a quit date, use of a contract with a specified quit date, reinforcing correspondence (letters mailed from clinical/study staff congratulating the patient on his or her decision to quit or on early success), providing information about the health risks of smoking, and so on.

National Committee for Quality Assurance (NCQA). Reviews and accredits managed care organizations, develops processes for measuring health plan performance, and disseminates information about quality so consumers can make informed choices (e.g., report cards like HEDIS).

Negative affect/depression component. A type of intervention designed to train patients to cope with negative affect after cessation. The intensity of the interventions in this category may vary from prolonged counseling to the simple provision of information about coping with negative moods. To receive this code, interventions targeted depressed mood, not simply stress. Interventions aimed at teaching subjects to cope with stressors were coded as problemsolving. When it was unclear whether an intervention was directed at negative affect/depression or at psychosocial stress, problemsolving was the default code.

Nicotine replacement therapy (NRT). Refers to a medication containing nicotine that is intended to promote smoking cessation. There are four nicotine replacement therapy delivery systems currently approved for use in the United States. These include nicotine chewing gum, nicotine inhaler, nicotine patch, and nicotine nasal spray.

Nortriptyline. A tricyclic antidepressant identified by the guideline panel as a second-line pharmacotherapy for smoking cessation. The FDA has not approved nortriptyline as a smoking cessation aid.

Odds ratio. The odds of an outcome on one variable, given a certain status on another variable(s). This ratio expresses the increase in risk of a given outcome if the variable is present.

Oral mucosa. The mucous membranes that line the mouth.

Person-to-person intervention. In-person, or face-to-face, contact between a clinician and a patient(s) for the purpose of tobacco use intervention or assessment.

Physiological feedback. A treatment by which a clinician provides to a tobacco user biological information, such as spirometry readings, carbon monoxide readings, or genetic susceptibility information, for the purpose of increasing abstinence from tobacco use.

Point prevalence. A measure of tobacco abstinence based on smoking/tobacco use occurrence within a set time period (usually 7 days) prior to a followup assessment.

Practical counseling (problemsolving/skills training). Refers to a tobacco use treatment in which tobacco users are trained to identify and cope with events or problems that increase the likelihood of their tobacco use. For example, quitters might be trained to anticipate stressful events and to use coping skills such as distraction or deep breathing to cope with an urge to smoke. Related and similar interventions are coping skill training, relapse prevention, and stress management.

Primary care clinician. A clinician (e.g., in medicine, nursing, psychology, pharmacology, dentistry/oral health, physical, occupational, and respiratory therapy) who provides basic health care services for problems other than tobacco use per se. Primary care providers are encouraged to identify tobacco users and to intervene, regardless of whether tobacco use is the patient's presenting problem.

Proactive telephone counseling. Treatment initiated by a clinician who telephones and counsels the patient over the telephone.

Propranolol. A beta-adrenergic blocker often used as an antihypertensive medication.

Psychosocial interventions. Refers to intervention strategies that are designed to increase tobacco abstinence rates due to psychological or social support mechanisms. These interventions comprise such treatment strategies as counseling, self-help, and behavioral treatment like rapid smoking and contingency contracting.

Purchaser. A corporation, company, Government agency, or other consortium that purchases health care benefits for a group of individuals.

Quit day. The day of a given cessation attempt during which a patient tries to abstain totally from tobacco use. Also refers to a motivational intervention, whereby a patient commits to quit tobacco use on a specified day.

Randomized controlled trial. For the purposes of this guideline, a study in which subjects are assigned to conditions on the basis of chance, and where at least one of the conditions is a control or comparison condition.

Reference group. In meta-analyses, refers to the group against which other groups are compared (i.e., a comparison or control group).

Relaxation/breathing. An intervention strategy in which patients are trained in relaxation techniques. Interventions using meditation, breathing exercises, and so on, fit this category. This category should be distinguished from the category of problemsolving, which includes a much wider range of stress-reduction/ management strategies.

Restricted Environmental Stimulation Therapy. Also known as REST. A treatment involving the use of sensory deprivation to promote abstinence from tobacco use.

Second-hand smoke. Also known as environmental tobacco smoke (ETS). The smoke inhaled by an individual not actively engaged in smoking but due to exposure to ambient tobacco smoke.

Second-line pharmacotherapy for tobacco dependence. Second-line medications are pharmacotherapies for which there is evidence of efficacy for treating tobacco dependence, but they have a more limited role than first-line medications because: (1) the FDA has not approved them for a tobacco dependence treatment indication, and (2) there are more concerns about potential side effects than exist with first-line medications. Second-line treatments should be considered for use on a case-by-case basis after first-line treatments have been used or considered.

Self-help. An intervention strategy in which the patient uses a nonpharmacologic physical aid to achieve abstinence from tobacco. Self-help strategies typically involve little contact with a clinician, although some strategies (e.g., hotline/ helpline) involve patient-initiated contact. Examples of types of self-help materials include: pamphlets/booklets/mailings/manuals; videos; audios; referrals to 12-step programs; mass media community-level interventions; lists of community programs; reactive telephone hotlines/helplines; and computer programs/Internet.

Self-selected. Refers to a patient population that seeks or agrees to participate in a tobacco use treatment. May be contrasted with an "all-comers" population in which treatment is provided without the patient actively seeking it (see "all-comers").

Serum cotinine. Level of cotinine in the blood. Cotinine is nicotine's major metabolite, which has a significantly longer half-life than nicotine. This is often used to estimate a patient's tobacco/nicotine self-administration prior to quitting, and to confirm abstinence self-reports during followup. Cotinine is commonly measured in urine and saliva.

Serum nicotine. Level of nicotine in the blood. This is often used to assess a patient's tobacco/nicotine self-administration prior to quitting, and to confirm abstinence self-reports during followup. Nicotine is commonly measured in urine and saliva.

Silver acetate. Silver acetate reacts with cigarette smoke to produce an unpleasant taste and has been investigated as a deterrent to smoking.

Smokeless tobacco. Any used form of unburned tobacco, including chewing tobacco and snuff.

Specialized assessments. Refers to assessment of patient characteristics, such as nicotine dependence and motivation for quitting, that may allow clinicians to tailor interventions to the needs of the individual patient.

Starter kits. Self-help materials and/or programs usually provided by a pharmaceutical company to assist patients in successfully quitting smoking while using a pharmaceutical medication.

Stepped-care. The practice of initiating treatment with a low-intensity intervention and then exposing treatment failures to successively more intense interventions.

Tailored interventions. Tailored interventions are based on a dimension, or a subset of dimensions, of the individual (i.e. weight concerns, dependency, etc.). See also individualized interventions.

Targeted interventions. Targeted interventions are defined as interventions that focus on particular populations (i.e., racial groups, women, etc.).

Telephone hotline/helpline. A reactive telephone line dedicated to over-the-phone smoking intervention. A hotline/helpline treatment occurs when a hotline/helpline number is provided to a patient, or a referral to a hotline/helpline is made. The key distinction between a hotline/helpline and proactive telephone counseling is that in the former the patient must initiate clinical contact.

Tobacco dependence specialists. These specialists typically provide intensive tobacco interventions. Specialists are not defined by their professional affiliation or by the field in which they trained. Rather, specialists view tobacco dependence treatment as a primary professional role. Specialists possess the skills, knowledge, and training to provide efficacious interventions across a range of intensities, and often are affiliated with programs offering intensive treatment interventions or services.

Transdermal nicotine. Refers to delivery of nicotine by diffusion through the skin. Often used as a synonym for "nicotine patch."

Treatment matching. Differential assignment of patients to treatments based on the patient's pretreatment characteristics. Treatment matching is based on the notion that particular types of tobacco users are most likely to benefit from particular types of treatments.

Weight/diet/nutrition component. An intervention strategy designed to address weight gain or concerns about weight gain. Interventions that teach nutrition/diet/weight management strategies, incorporate daily/weekly weight monitoring (for reasons other than routine data collection), require or suggest energy intake maintenance/reduction, and/or convey nutritional information/tips/counseling receive this code.

Contributors

Guideline Panel

Michael C. Fiore, MD, MPH
Panel Chair
Professor, Department of Medicine
Director, Center for Tobacco Research and Intervention
University of Wisconsin Medical School
Madison, Wisconsin

Dr. Fiore completed medical school at Northwestern University and his internal medicine training at Boston City Hospital. His postgraduate education included a Master of Public Health in Epidemiology from Harvard University. Dr. Fiore received additional training in epidemiology as an Epidemic Intelligence Service (EIS) Officer for the Centers for Disease Control and Prevention, where he completed a Preventive Medicine residency program. Dr. Fiore worked as a medical epidemiologist at the U.S. Office on Smoking and Health, where he contributed to a wide range of national research, educational, and policy projects to control the epidemic of tobacco-related diseases. He is Director of the Center for Tobacco Research and Intervention and a Professor of Medicine at the University of Wisconsin Medical School. At the University of Wisconsin, Dr. Fiore is clinically active, treating patients both in internal medicine and for smoking cessation. He served as Chair of the Agency for Health Care Policy and Research panel that produced the *Smoking Cessation Clinical Practice Guideline No. 18*. Currently, he serves as Director of a Robert Wood Johnson Foundation National Program Office, Addressing Tobacco in Managed Care.

William C. Bailey, MD, FACP, FCCP
Director, Lung Health Center
University of Alabama at Birmingham
Birmingham, Alabama

Dr. Bailey graduated from Tulane University Medical School in 1965. He is a Diplomate of the American Board of Internal Medicine in both Internal Medicine and Pulmonary Disease, having received certified specialty training in these disciplines at Tulane University Medical Center and Charity Hospital of Louisiana. He has been on the faculty of the University of Alabama at Birmingham (UAB) since 1973. He has practiced medicine, taught, performed research, and been involved in administrative endeavors for his entire career. He has served on the Board of Directors of the American Thoracic Society and also has served on the Council of the National Heart, Lung, and Blood Institute. He has been a member of many editorial review boards of peer-reviewed journals and has served as a frequent scientific reviewer of both scientific articles and peer-reviewed research. He currently holds the Eminent Scholar Chair in Pulmonary Diseases while also being the Director of the UAB Lung Health Center, which is devoted to research in the prevention of lung disease.

Stuart J. Cohen, EdD
Canyon Ranch Endowed Chair
University of Arizona Prevention Center
Tucson, Arizona

Dr. Cohen received his doctorate in Educational Foundations/Psychology from the University of Rochester. For the past 21 years, he has received grants to improve the quality of ambulatory primary care from the National Institutes of Health, the Centers for Disease Control and Prevention, and the Agency for Healthcare Research and Quality. He has published extensively on health promotion and disease prevention interventions directed at both health care providers and patients. His research on methods to improve physician and dentist interventions in smoking cessation showed the importance of having office systems that include reminders for delivery of preventive services.

Sally Faith Dorfman, MD, MSHSA
Director, Division of Public Health and Education
The Medical Society of the State of NY
Lake Success, NY 11042

Dr. Dorfman holds a degree in economics from Harvard/Radcliffe College, a master's degree in Health Services Administration, and an MD from Stanford University. She trained in reproductive health epidemiology as an Epidemic Intelligence Service (EIS) Officer at the Centers for Disease Control and Prevention. She is board certified both in obstetrics and gynecology and in public health/general preventive medicine. Dr. Dorfman has consulted for State, regional, national, and international organizations and was Commissioner of Health for Orange County, New York, from 1988 to 1994. Also, she has published and presented extensively for professional and lay audiences, serves as reviewer for several peer-review journals, and is the recipient of numerous honors and awards. Dr. Dorfman is Director of the Division of Public Health and Education of the Medical Society of the State of New York, and is clinically active as a gynecologist.

Michael G. Goldstein, MD
Associate Director, Clinical Education and Research
Bayer Institute for Health Care Communication
West Haven, Connecticut

Dr. Goldstein is board certified in Internal Medicine and Psychiatry and currently serves as an Associate Director for Clinical Education and Research at the Bayer Institute for Health Care Communication in West Haven, Connecticut. Also, he is an Investigator at the Center for Behavioral and Preventive Medicine at the Miriam Hospital in Providence, Rhode Island, and an Adjunct Professor of

Psychiatry and Human Behavior at Brown University School of Medicine. Dr. Goldstein's primary research interests have included developing interventions to enhance the delivery of smoking cessation in primary care settings and testing the efficacy of combined behavioral and pharmacologic interventions for smoking cessation. Dr. Goldstein has served as a member of the Task Force on Nicotine Dependence of the American Psychiatric Association (APA) and also has served on the APA Nicotine Dependence Practice Guideline Panel. He has published extensively in the areas of behavioral medicine, smoking cessation, and health care communication.

Ellen R. Gritz, PhD
Professor and Chair
Department of Behavioral Science
University of Texas
M.D. Anderson Cancer Center
Houston, Texas

Dr. Gritz is a licensed psychologist and an established leader in cancer prevention and control research. She has published extensively on cigarette smoking behavior, including prevention, cessation, pharmacologic mechanisms, effects on weight, and special issues of women and other high-risk groups (e.g., ethnic minorities, adolescents, and medical populations). Other areas of interest include adherence to cancer control regimens, genetic testing and counseling for hereditary cancers, and quality of life in cancer survivors. Dr. Gritz has served on the National Cancer Policy Board and the Board on Health Promotion and Disease Prevention of the Institute of Medicine.

Richard B. Heyman, MD
Former Chair, Committee on Substance Abuse
American Academy of Pediatrics
Cincinnati, Ohio

A graduate of the Columbia University College of Physicians and Surgeons, Dr. Heyman practices pediatric and adolescent medicine and serves on the faculty of the Division of Adolescent Medicine at Children's Hospital Medical Center in Cincinnati, Ohio. He is a consultant to several adolescent chemical dependency programs and lectures widely in the area of substance abuse. As former chairman of the Committee on Substance Abuse of the American Academy of Pediatrics, he has played a major role in the creation of the Academy's educational programs and materials, as well as the development of policy in the area of alcohol, tobacco, and other drug abuse.

Carlos Roberto Jaén, MD, PhD
Associate Professor and Vice-Chair
Department of Family Medicine
Director, Center for Urban Research in Primary Care
State University of New York at Buffalo
Buffalo, New York

Dr. Jaén completed medical school at the State University of New York at Buffalo (UB), and his Family Practice Residency and Primary Care Research Fellowship at Case Western Reserve University in Cleveland, Ohio. His graduate education included a PhD in Epidemiology with a concentration in Tobacco Control at Roswell Park Cancer Institute. Dr. Jaén is Director of the Center for Urban Research in Primary Care, Associate Professor and Vice Chair for Research and Development at UB's Department of Family Medicine, and Co-Director of the American Academy of Family Physician's funded Research Center to Evaluate the Value of Family Practice. Dr. Jaén, active in primary care and public health research since 1985, has authored more than 30 publications on smoking cessation and related subjects, such as clinical preventive service delivery and access to care by the urban poor. In 1995, he received a Generalist Physician Faculty Scholar Award by the Robert Wood Johnson Foundation to study asthma among the urban poor in Buffalo. He directs and practices at the Niagara Family Health Center, located in the heart of Buffalo's Puerto Rican community.

Thomas E. Kottke, MD, MSPH
Professor of Medicine
Consultant, Department of Internal Medicine
Division of Cardiovascular Diseases
Mayo Clinic
Rochester, Minnesota

Dr. Kottke is a clinical cardiologist, epidemiologist, and health services researcher whose primary interest is describing, defining, and overcoming the barriers to the delivery of clinical preventive services. He has published widely on the evidence that clinical support systems are necessary for physicians and other health care professionals to provide preventive services to the patients they serve. Dr. Kottke was a member of the first U.S. Preventive Services Task Force.

Harry A. Lando, PhD
Professor, Division of Epidemiology
School of Public Health
University of Minnesota
Minneapolis, Minnesota

Dr. Lando has worked in the field of smoking cessation since 1969. He has published extensively in this area and was a scientific editor of the 1988 *Report of the Surgeon General: Nicotine Addiction*. His research has focused primarily on the development of effective multicomponent behavioral programs for smoking cessation. He has received numerous awards for his work and has consulted actively with Federal and voluntary agencies, including the National Cancer Institute; the Centers for Disease Control and Prevention; the American Cancer Society; the American Lung Association; the National Heart, Lung, and Blood Institute; and the National Institute on Drug Abuse.

Robert E. Mecklenburg, DDS, MPH
Coordinator, Tobacco and Oral Health Initiatives
Tobacco Control Research Branch, National Cancer Institute
Potomac, Maryland

Dr. Mecklenburg is a Diplomate of the American Board of Dental Public Health. He organizes and manages dental affairs for the National Cancer Institute's Tobacco Control Research Branch and is the tobacco-related research and development advisor for the National Institute of Dental and Craniofacial Research's Office of Science Policy and Analysis. He chairs the National Dental Tobacco-Free Steering Committee and is Vice-Chairman of the Dentistry Against Tobacco Section/Tobacco and Oral Health Committee of the FDI World Dental Federation. He chaired the committee on non-cancer oral effects of tobacco for the first Surgeon General's report on smokeless tobacco. He is the principal author of the NCI publications, *Tobacco Effects in the Mouth* and *How to Help Your Patients Stop Using Tobacco: A Manual for the Oral Health Team.* Dr. Mecklenburg has published and lectured widely in the United States and abroad about dental professionals' involvement in the creation of a tobacco-free society.

Patricia Dolan Mullen, DrPH
Professor/Behavioral Sciences
School of Public Health
University of Texas/Houston
Houston, Texas

Dr. Mullen is Professor of Behavioral Sciences as well as Training Director and a Senior Investigator at the Center for Health Promotion Research and Development. She has received research grants to study smoking cessation during pregnancy, and she has conducted meta-analyses on this and other topics. She has served on the Expert Panel on the Content of Prenatal Care and on research advisory panels and boards for the National Institutes of Health, the Centers for Disease Control and Prevention, the American Cancer Society, and other national and international organizations. In addition, Dr. Mullen was invited to write the section on smoking cessation during pregnancy for the 2000 *Surgeon General's Report on Women and Smoking.*

Louise M. Nett, RN, RRT
Research Associate, Executive Board Member
National Lung Health Education Program
Denver, Colorado

Ms. Nett currently is a research associate at the HealthONE Center at Presbyterian/St. Lukes Hospital and focuses on the early detection of chronic obstructive lung disease and lung cancer, and smoking cessation. Her early work focused on critical care, pulmonary rehabilitation, and oxygen therapy. She is a member of the American Thoracic Society, the American Association for Respiratory Care, the Society for Research on Nicotine and Tobacco, and the American College of Chest Physicians. Ms. Nett has published and taught extensively on the mentioned topics, and she is co-editor of the newsletter *Lung Cancer Frontiers*. She has received numerous awards and has consulted and lectured internationally.

Lawrence Robinson, MD, MPH
Deputy Health Commissioner
Philadelphia Department of Public Health
Health Promotion/Disease Prevention
Philadelphia, Pennsylvania

A graduate of Harvard College, Dr. Robinson received his MD from the University of Pennsylvania School of Medicine. He received his MPH and completed a residency in preventive medicine at Johns Hopkins University. He was a resident and faculty member at Rush and Columbia University while performing his internal medicine training. As Deputy Commissioner for Health Promotion/ Disease Prevention for the Philadelphia Department of Public Health, Dr. Robinson is responsible for the development, planning, implementation, and evaluation of various programs delivering medical, chronic disease prevention, and health education services. Local anti-tobacco projects include banning vending machines, assisting the county jail move to a smoke-free environment, Nicotrol Patch replacement, and the American Cancer Society Fresh Start Program. This train-the-trainer program was provided to the mentally ill and other targeted populations. Dr. Robinson also is a board member of the Pennsylvania American Cancer Society and Chairman of the State Tobacco Core Team. He is a member of various groups, organizations, and agencies in the community working on issues such as the State Tobacco Settlement (No Butts/Do the Right Thing) and smoking prevention for youth and special populations such as pregnant women.

Maxine L. Stitzer, PhD
Professor, Department of Psychiatry and Behavioral Sciences
Behavioral Biology Research Center
Johns Hopkins/Bayview Medical Center
Baltimore, Maryland

Dr. Stitzer received her PhD in Psychology and training in psychopharmacology from the University of Michigan. At Johns Hopkins University, she has developed a varied and extensive grant-supported research program focusing on both pharmacological and behavioral approaches to the treatment of substance abuse. Her many publications reflect active research interests in both illicit drug abuse and tobacco dependence. She has been president of the Division on Psychopharmacology and Substance Abuse of the American Psychological Association and has served on the Board of Directors of the College on Problems of Drug Dependence.

Anthony C. Tommasello, MS
Director, Office of Substance Abuse Studies
University of Maryland School of Pharmacy
Baltimore, Maryland

Mr. Tommasello, a pharmacist, is an Associate Professor of Clinical Pharmacy at the University of Maryland School of Pharmacy, and Director, Office of Substance Abuse Studies, which he founded. He has worked in the addiction field since 1973 and acquired advanced degrees in both pharmacology and epidemiology, specializing in drug abuse and addiction. He is active in clinical research and treatment in addictions and has created educational programs that have served as national models for pharmacists and other health and human service providers. He is the president of the Maryland Pharmacists' Rehabilitation Committee, which provides advocacy and treatment access for impaired pharmacists. He has published in the areas of general principles of assessment and treatment, methadone maintenance care, and adolescent drug abuse and addiction. Mr. Tommasello is a PhD candidate in Policy Sciences at University of Maryland–Baltimore Campus, where his focus has been on health policy analysis. His dissertation is entitled "The Effects of State Policies on Addiction Intervention in the Health Professions: The Case of Pharmacy."

Louise Villejo, MPH, CHES
Director, Patient Education Office
Office of Public Affairs
University of Texas M.D. Anderson Cancer Center
Houston, Texas

As the Director of the Patient Education Office at the M.D. Anderson Cancer Center, Ms. Villejo is responsible for the design, implementation, evaluation, and management of institution-wide patient and family education programs. She has designed and implemented Patient/Family Learning Centers as well as award-winning disease specific patient education programs and produced more than 100 patient education print materials and videotapes. For the past 10 years, she has served on the National Cancer Institute's Advisory Boards and Patient Education Network's Steering Committee as well as on numerous other Federal and private advisory and planning boards and committees. Ms. Villejo's publications include articles on cancer patient education and cultural diversity in health care.

Mary Ellen Wewers, PhD, MPH, RN
Professor
College of Nursing
Ohio State University
Columbus, Ohio

Dr. Wewers, an Adult Nurse Practitioner, received her PhD in Nursing from the University of Maryland at Baltimore and an MPH from Harvard University. She has been funded by the National Institutes of Health (NIH) to investigate reinforcement for nicotine in both human and animal models of dependence. Her current NIH-funded research examines nurse-managed tobacco cessation interventions in underserved groups. Dr. Wewers is past Chair of the Nursing Assembly of the American Thoracic Society and a past member of the American Thoracic Society's Board of Directors. She serves as co-director of the Nursing Center for Tobacco Intervention at Ohio State University.

Senior Consultants

Timothy Baker, PhD
Senior Scientific Consultant
Professor, Department of Psychology
Associate Director, Center for Tobacco
  Research and Intervention
University of Wisconsin Medical
  School
Madison, Wisconsin

Victor Hasselblad, PhD
Statistical Methodologist
Duke Clinical Research Institute
Duke University
Durham, North Carolina

Other Consultants

Marc Manley, MD, MPH
Executive Director, Center for Tobacco
  Reduction and Health Improvement
Blue Cross and Blue Shield of
  Minnesota
St. Paul, Minnesota

John Mullahy, PhD
Professor, Department of Preventive
  Medicine
Department of Economics
University of Wisconsin, Madison
Madison, Wisconsin

David L. Schriger, MD, MPH
Associate Professor
UCLA School of Medicine
UCLA Emergency Medicine Center
Los Angeles, California

David W. Wetter, PhD
Associate Scientific Advisor
Center for Health Studies
Seattle, Washington

Project Staff

Brion J. Fox, JD
Project Director
Center for Tobacco Research and
  Intervention
University of Wisconsin Medical
  School
Madison, Wisconsin

Bridget C. Whisler
Project Manager
Center for Tobacco Research and
  Intervention
University of Wisconsin Medical
  School
Madison, Wisconsin

Sam Welsch
Senior Research Associate
Center for Tobacco Research and
  Intervention
University of Wisconsin Medical
  School
Madison, Wisconsin

Megan Piper, MA
Senior Research Associate
Center for Tobacco Research and
  Intervention
University of Wisconsin Medical
  School
Madison, Wisconsin

Silvia Kang
Project Research Associate
Center for Tobacco Research and
  Intervention
University of Wisconsin Medical
  School
Madison, Wisconsin

Rebecca Boex
Project Research Associate
Center for Tobacco Research and
  Intervention
University of Wisconsin Medical
  School
Madison, Wisconsin

Additional Project Staff

Kylee Carolfi
Mara Cvejic
Karin Christoph
Jackie Grove
Jason Horowitz
Ann Schensky
Melanie Schrank
Natalie Syty
Carolina Ugaz
Mark Zehner
Center for Tobacco Research and
  Intervention
University of Wisconsin Medical
  School
Madison, Wisconsin

Guideline Consortium Representatives

Agency for Healthcare Research and Quality
Rockville, Maryland

Douglas B. Kamerow, MD, MPH
Director
Center for Practice and Technology
  Assessment

Ernestine W. Murray, RN, MAS
Panel Project Officer
Center for Practice and Technology
  Assessment

Harriett V. Bennett
Public Affairs Specialist
Office of Health Care Information

Sandra Katz Cummings
Managing Editor
Office of Health Care Information

Centers for Disease Control and Prevention
Atlanta, Georgia

Corinne G. Husten, MD, MPH
Medical Officer
Office on Smoking and Health
National Center for Chronic Disease
  Prevention and Health Promotion

Cathy Melvin, PhD, MPH
Chief, Program Services and
  Development Branch
Division of Reproductive Health
National Center for Chronic Disease
  Prevention and Health Promotion

National Cancer Institute
Bethesda, Maryland

Glen D. Morgan, PhD
Tobacco Control Research Branch
Rockville, Maryland

National Heart, Lung, and Blood Institute
Bethesda, Maryland

Glen Bennett, MPH
Coordinator, Advance Technologies
  Applications in Health Education
  Programs
Office of Prevention, Education, and
  Control

National Institute on Drug Abuse
Rockville, Maryland

Stephen Heishman, PhD
Senior Investigator
Clinical Pharmacology and
  Therapeutics Branch
Baltimore, Maryland

The Robert Wood Johnson Foundation
Princeton, New Jersey

C. Tracy Orleans, PhD
Senior Scientist

Center for Tobacco Research and Intervention
University of Wisconsin Medical School
Madison, Wisconsin

Douglas Jorenby, PhD
University of Wisconsin Medical
  School

Contract Support

The Scientific Consulting Group, Inc.
Gaithersburg, Maryland

Marcia Feinleib
Project Director

Maria Osvald
Managing Editor

Mark Searles
Production Manager

Article Reviewers

Brion J. Fox, JD
Rebecca Boex
Mara Cvejic
Silvia Kang
Natalie Syty
Carolina Ugaz
Sam Welsch
Center for Tobacco Research and
  Intervention
University of Wisconsin Medical
  School
Madison, Wisconsin

Peer Reviewers

Jasjits S. Ahluwalia, MD, MPH MS
Vice Chair and Director of Research
Preventive Medicine
University of Kansas Medical Center
Kansas City, Missouri

Frederic Bass, MD, DSC
Director, BC Doctors Stop-Smoking
  Program and Specialist in Clinical
  Preventive Health Care
Vancouver, BC Canada

Terry L. Bazzarre, PhD
Staff Scientist
American Heart Association
Dallas, Texas

Michele Bloch, MD, PhD
Medical Officer
Tobacco Control Research Branch
National Cancer Institute
Rockville, Maryland

Alan Blum, MD
Founder and Chairman
Doctors Ought to Care
DOC Tobacco Archive and
  International Resource Center
Houston, Texas

Thomas H. Brandon, PhD
Director, Tobacco Research
H. Lee Moffitt Cancer Center Institute
Tampa, Florida

Joan Brewster, PhD
Assistant Professor
Department of Public Health Sciences
University of Toronto
Toronto, Ontario, Canada

David M. Burns, MD
Professor of Medicine
Division of Pulmonary and Critical
  Care
University of California-San Diego
  School of Medicine
San Diego, California

Janet Chapin, RN, MPH
Director, Division of Women's Health
  Issues
The American College of Obstetricians
  and Gynecologists
Washington, DC

Helene Cole, MD
Senior Editor, JAMA
American Medical Association
Chicago, Illinois

William A. Corrigall, PhD
Research Scientist
Center for Addiction and Mental
  Health
Nicotine and Tobacco Dependence
  Program
Toronto, Ontario, Canada

David R. Coultas, MD
Professor and Chief, Epidemiology and
  Preventive Medicine
University of New Mexico Health
  Sciences Center
Department of Internal Medicine
Epidemiology and Cancer Control
  Program
Albuquerque, New Mexico

Susan J. Curry, PhD
Director, Center for Health Studies
Group Health Cooperative
Seattle, Washington

Ronald M. Davis
Director, Center for Health Promotion
Henry Ford Health System
Detroit, Michigan

Jane Delgado, PhD, MS
President and CEO
National Coalition of Hispanic Health
  and Human Services
Washington, DC

Karl O. Fagerstrom, PhD
Director
Pharmacy
S-25109 Helsingborg, Sweden

Sam P. Giordano, MBA, RRT
Executive Director
American Association for Respiratory
  Care
Dallas, Texas

Elbert D. Glover, PhD
Professor, Department of Behavioral
  Medicine and Psychiatry
West Virginia School of Medicine
Mary Babb Randolph Cancer Center
Morgantown, West Virginia

Thomas J. Glynn, PhD
Director, Cancer Science and Trends
American Cancer Society
Washington, DC

Sharon M. Hall, PhD
Professor and Vice-Chair, Psychiatry
  Department
University of California-San Francisco
San Francisco, California

Dorothy K. Hatsukami, PhD
Professor and Consulting Psychologist
Department of Psychiatry
University of Minnesota
Minneapolis, Minnesota

Jack E. Henningfield, PhD
Vice President
Research and Health Policy
Pinney Associates
Bethesda, Maryland

Thomas P. Houston, MD
Director
Department of Preventive Medicine
  and Environmental Health
American Medical Association
Chicago, Illinois

John R. Hughes, MD
Professor, Department of Psychiatry
University of Vermont
Burlington, Vermont

Martin J. Jarvis, MPhD
Imperial Cancer Research Fund
Department of Epidemiology and
  Public Health
University College London
London, England

J. Andrew Johnston, PharmD
Head, Psychiatry Clinical Development
Glaxo Wellcome, Inc.
Research Triangle Park, North
  Carolina

Nancy Kaufman, MS, RN
Vice President
The Robert Wood Johnson Foundation
Princeton, New Jersey

Robert C. Klesges, PhD
Executive Director
University of Memphis Prevention
  Center
Memphis, Tennessee

Connie L. Kohler, DrPH
Assistant Professor
School of Public Health
University of Alabama at Birmingham
Birmingham, Alabama

B. Wain Kong, MD
Executive Director
Association of Black Cardiologists
Atlanta, Georgia

Eva Kralikova, MD, PhD
First Faculty of Medicine
Charles University
Prague, Czech Republic

Edward Lichtenstein, PhD
Research Scientist
Oregon Research Institute
Eugene, Oregon

Kathleen Lindell, RN, MSN
Program Director
The PENN Quit Smoking Program
University of Pennsylvania
Philadelphia, Pennsylvania

Daniel R. Longo, ScD
Professor, Family and Community
  Medicine
University of Missouri-Columbia
Columbia, Missouri

Jerold R. Mande
Deputy Assistant Secretary
Occupational Safety and Health
  Administration
U.S. Department of Labor
Washington, DC

Timothy McAfee, MD, MPH
Director, Center for Health Promotion
and Disease Prevention
Group Health Cooperative of Puget
  Sound
Seattle, Washington

Daniel E. McGoldrick, MA
Director, Research
Campaign for Tobacco-Free Kids
Washington, DC

Norman Montalto, DO
Associate Professor, Family Medicine
Director, Freedom from Tobacco
  Program
Robert C. Byrd Health Sciences
  Center
West Virginia University/Charleston
  Division
Charleston, West Virginia

Mildred S. Morse, JD
Director, National Tobacco
  Independence Campaign
Morse Enterprises, Inc.
Silver Spring, Maryland

Judith K. Ockene, PhD, MEd
Professor of Medicine
Director, Division of Preventive and
  Behavioral Medicine
University of Massachusetts Medical
  School
Worcester, Massachusetts

Debra J. Ossip-Klein, PhD
Research Associate Professor of
  Community and Preventive Medicine
  and Oncology
Director, Smoking Research Program
University of Rochester Cancer Center
Rochester, New York

Pamela H. Payne
Project Director, Tobacco ROAD
National Medical Association
Washington, DC

Thomas A. Pearson, MD, MPH, PhD
Professor and Chair of Community and
  Preventive Medicine
University of Rochester
Rochester, New York

Kenneth A. Perkins, PhD
Professor of Psychiatry
Western Psychiatric Institute and Clinic
University of Pittsburgh
Pittsburgh, Pennsylvania

John P. Pierce, PhD
Sam M. Walton Professor for Cancer
  Research
UCSD Cancer Center
University of California-San Diego
San Diego, California

Donald Pine, MD
Family Practice Physician
Health System Minnesota
Minneapolis, Minnesota

Patricia G. Porter, RN, MPH, CHES
Director, Project Development
Integrating Medicine and Public Health
  Program
UCSF Institute for Health and Aging
California Department of Health
  Services
San Francisco, California

Stephen I. Rennard, MD
Professor of Medicine
University of Nebraska Medical Center
Omaha, Nebraska

Nancy A. Rigotti, MD
Director, Tobacco Research and
  Treatment Center
Harvard Medical School
Massachusetts General Hospital
Boston, Massachusetts

Barbara K. Rimer, DrPH
Division of Cancer Control and
  Population Sciences
National Cancer Institute
Rockville, Maryland

William A. Robinson, MD, MPH
Director, Center for Quality
Chief Medical Officer
Health Resources and Services
  Administration
Department of Health and Human
  Services
Rockville, Maryland

Jacqueline Royce, PhD
President, Royce Associates
Atlantic Highlands, New Jersey

Helen H. Schauffler, PhD, MSPH
Associate Professor and Director
Center for Health and Public Policy
  Studies
University of California-Berkeley
School of Public Health
Berkeley, California

Manuel Schydlower, MD
Professor of Pediatrics
Assistant Dean for Medical Education
Texas Tech Health Sciences Center
El Paso, Texas

Roger Secker-Walker, MB, FRCP
Professor Emeritus
University of Vermont
Burlington, Vermont

Herbert Severson, PhD
Senior Research Scientist
Oregon Research Institute
Eugene, Oregon

Saul Shiffman, PhD
Professor of Psychology
University of Pittsburgh
Pittsburgh, Pennsylvania

John Slade, MD
Professor
Department of Environment and
  Community Medicine
The Robert Wood Johnson Medical
  School
New Brunswick, New Jersey

Leif I. Solberg, MD
Director for Care Improvement
  Research
Group Health Foundation
Minneapolis, Minnesota

Anne N. Thorndike, MD
Instructor of Medicine
Harvard Medical School and
  Massachusetts General Hospital
Boston, Massachusetts

Phillip K. Tonnesen, MD
Chief of Department
Department of Pulmonary Disease
Gentofte Amts Hospital
Copenhagen, Denmark

Kenneth E. Warner, PhD
Richard D. Remington Collegiate
  Professor
University of Michigan School of
  Public Health
Ann Arbor, Michigan

Barbara Widmar, MA
Manager, Health Education
  Department
American Academy of Family
  Physicians
Leawood, Kansas

Richard Windsor, MS, MPH, PhD
Research Professor
Department of Human Studies
University of Alabama at Birmingham
Birmingham, Alabama

Douglas Ziedonis, MD, MPH
Director, Division of Addiction
  Psychiatry
Department of Psychiatry
The Robert Wood Johnson Medical
  School
Piscataway, New Jersey

Appendixes

Appendix A: Helpful Web Site Addresses

The inclusion of Web sites in this appendix is intended to assist readers in finding additional information regarding the treatment of tobacco use and dependence and does not constitute endorsement of the contents of any particular site.

Addressing Tobacco in Managed Care: www.aahp.org/atmc.htm

Agency for Healthcare Research and Quality: www.ahrq.gov

American Academy of Family Physicians: www.aafp.org

American Cancer Society: www.cancer.org

American Legacy Foundation: www.americanlegacy.org

American Psychological Association: www.apa.org

National Cancer Institute: www.nci.nih.gov

National Center for Tobacco-Free Kids: www.tobaccofreekids.org

National Guideline Clearinghouse: www.guideline.gov

National Heart, Lung, and Blood Institute: www.nhlbi.nih.gov/index.htm

National Institute on Drug Abuse: www.nida.nih.gov/NIDAHome1.html

Office on Smoking and Health at the Centers for Disease Control and Prevention: www.cdc.gov/tobacco

Office on Smoking and Health at the Centers for Disease Control and Prevention: State highlights including lists of State tobacco control contacts: www.cdc.gov/ tobacco/statehi/statehi.htm

Society for Research on Nicotine and Tobacco: www.srnt.org

World Health Organization: www.who.int

Appendix B: Coding Information Regarding the Diagnosis of and Billing for Tobacco Dependence Treatment

Coding for the Treatment of Tobacco Use

Clinicians, clinic administrators, and health care delivery systems require appropriate diagnostic and billing codes for the documentation of reimbursement for tobacco dependence treatment. Information on such codes may help address a common clinical concern regarding the treatment of tobacco dependent patients: it is difficult to accurately document and obtain reimbursement for this treatment.

Although examples of such codes are provided below, clinicians and billing coders may use other diagnostic and reimbursement codes to document and obtain payment for this medical treatment. Additionally, it is incumbent on the clinician to ensure that appropriate billing guidelines are followed and to recognize that reimbursement of these codes may vary by payor or benefits package. For example, although psychiatric therapeutic codes appropriate for treating tobacco dependence exist, some payors or benefits packages have restrictions on mental health benefits. Similarly, reimbursement for preventive visits varies greatly among payors and benefits packages.

A systems-based approach will facilitate the understanding and use of such codes by clinicians. For example, various clinic or hospital meetings (e.g., business sessions, grand rounds, seminars, and coding in-service sessions) can explain and highlight the use of tobacco dependence codes for diagnosis and reimbursement. Additionally, these diagnostic codes can be preprinted on the billing and diagnostic coding sheets as a "check-off" rather than expect clinicians to recall and then manually document such treatment. Finally, clinicians can be reminded that counseling by itself is a reimbursable activity and can be billed for based on the number of minutes of counseling.

1. Diagnostic Codes (ICD-9-CM)

When clinicians provide treatment to patients dependent on tobacco, the following diagnostic codes can be used. They can be found in the ICD-9-CM (*International Classification of Diseases, 9th Revision, Clinical Modification*) coding manual under the section on Mental Disorders (290-319).

305.1 Tobacco Use Disorder. Cases in which tobacco is used to the detriment of a person's health or social functioning or in which there is tobacco dependence. Dependent is included here rather than under drug dependence because tobacco differs from other drugs of dependence in its psychotropic effect.

Tobacco Dependence—See Tobacco Use Disorder above. Excludes: History of tobacco use (V15.82).

V15.82 History of Tobacco Use. Excludes: Tobacco dependence (305.1).

2. Billing Codes

A number of billing codes may be used for reimbursement of the provision of tobacco dependence treatment. The examples provided fall under the general categories of preventive medicine treatments and psychiatric therapeutic procedures.

A. Preventive Medicine Treatments/Codes For Billing. Preventive medicine treatment codes allow for the billing of counseling and other activities related to risk factor reduction interventions. Given the recognition of tobacco use as a causal risk factor for cancer, coronary artery disease, chronic obstructive pulmonary diseases, and others, these billing codes are appropriate when treating tobacco dependence. These codes can be billed on the basis of time spent (in minutes) counseling the tobacco dependent patient. As with other counseling billing requirements, the clinicians must indicate as part of the note the number of minutes counseled (CT) and the total number of minutes (TT) treating the patient.

For preventive medicine services, billing codes are distinguished based on the age of the patient, whether it is a new or established patient, whether the counseling is individual or group, whether the treatment was part of a comprehensive preventive medicine examination (**codes 99383-99387**), or whether it was specific preventive medicine counseling to intervene with the risk factor of tobacco dependence. These billing codes can be used for initial and followup treatments of tobacco use. For comprehensive preventive medicine examinations, the term "comprehensive" is not synonymous with the comprehensive examination requirements in the evaluation and management service codes (**90201-90350**).

A1. Tobacco Dependence Treatment As Part Of The Initial Or Periodic Comprehensive Preventive Medicine Examination

New Patient

99383 Initial preventive medicine evaluation and management of an individual, including a comprehensive history, a comprehensive examination, and counseling/anticipatory guidance, to treat the risk factor of tobacco use and the ordering of appropriate laboratory/diagnostic procedures. Late childhood (age 5-11 years).

99384 Initial preventive medicine evaluation and management of an individual, including a comprehensive history, a comprehensive examination, and counseling/anticipatory guidance, to treat the risk factor of tobacco use and the ordering of appropriate laboratory/diagnostic procedures. Adolescent (age 12-17 years).

99385 Initial preventive medicine evaluation and management of an individual, including a comprehensive history, a comprehensive examination, and counseling/ anticipatory guidance, to treat the risk factor of tobacco use and the ordering of appropriate laboratory/diagnostic procedures. Adult (age 18-39 years).

99386 Initial preventive medicine evaluation and management of an individual, including a comprehensive history, a comprehensive examination, and counseling/ anticipatory guidance, to treat the risk factor of tobacco use and the ordering of appropriate laboratory/diagnostic procedures. Adult (age 40-64 years).

99387 Initial preventive medicine evaluation and management of an individual, including a comprehensive history, a comprehensive examination, and counseling/ anticipatory guidance, to treat the risk factor of tobacco use and the ordering of appropriate laboratory/diagnostic procedures. Adult (age 65 years and older).

Established Patient

99393 Periodic preventive medicine re-evaluation and management of an individual, including a comprehensive history, comprehensive examination, and counseling/anticipatory guidance, to treat the risk factor of tobacco use and the ordering of appropriate laboratory/diagnostic procedures. Established patient, late childhood (age 5-11 years).

99394 Periodic preventive medicine re-evaluation and management of an individual, including a comprehensive history, comprehensive examination, and counseling/anticipatory guidance, to treat the risk factor of tobacco use and the ordering of appropriate laboratory/diagnostic procedures. Established patient, adolescent (age 12-17 years).

99395 Periodic preventive medicine re-evaluation and management of an individual, including a comprehensive history, comprehensive examination, and counseling/anticipatory guidance, to treat the risk factor of tobacco use and the ordering of appropriate laboratory/diagnostic procedures. Established patient, adult (age 18-39 years).

99396 Periodic preventive medicine re-evaluation and management of an individual, including a comprehensive history, comprehensive examination, and counseling/anticipatory guidance, to treat the risk factor of tobacco use and the ordering of appropriate laboratory/diagnostic procedures. Established patient, adult (age 40-64 years).

99397 Periodic preventive medicine re-evaluation and management of an individual, including a comprehensive history, comprehensive examination, and counseling/anticipatory guidance, to treat the risk factor of tobacco use and the ordering of appropriate laboratory/diagnostic procedures. Established patient, adult (age 65 years and older).

A2. Tobacco Dependence Treatment as Specific Counseling and/or Risk Factor Reduction Intervention

These codes are used to report services provided to individuals at a separate encounter for the purpose of promoting health and preventing illness or injury. As such, they are appropriate for the specific treatment of tobacco use and dependence. They are appropriate for initial or followup tobacco dependence treatments (new or established patient).

For the specific preventive medicine counseling codes, the number of minutes counseled determined the level of billing (**codes 99400-99404** for 15 to 60 minutes of counseling).

Preventive Medicine, Individual Counseling

99401 Preventive medicine counseling and/or intervention to treat the risk factor of tobacco use provided to an individual (separate procedure); approximately 15 minutes.

99402 Preventive medicine counseling and/or intervention to treat the risk factor of tobacco use provided to an individual (separate procedure); approximately 30 minutes.

99403 Preventive medicine counseling and/or intervention to treat the risk factor of tobacco use provided to an individual (separate procedure); approximately 45 minutes.

99404 Preventive medicine counseling and/or intervention to treat the risk factor of tobacco use provided to an individual (separate procedure); approximately 60 minutes.

Preventive Medicine, Group Counseling

99411 Preventive medicine counseling and/or intervention to treat the risk factor of tobacco use provided to an individual (separate procedure); approximately 30 minutes.

99412 Preventive medicine counseling and/or intervention to treat the risk factor of tobacco use provided to an individual (separate procedure); approximately 60 minutes.

B. Psychiatric Therapeutic Procedures/Codes for Billing. The psychiatric therapeutic procedure billing codes are typically used for insight-oriented, behavior modifying and/or supported psychotherapy. This refers to the development of insight of affective understanding, the use of behavior modification techniques, the use of supportive interactions, the use of cognitive discussion of reality, or any combination of the above to provide therapeutic change. All of the counseling interventions for tobacco dependence demonstrated to be effective in this guideline would fall under these headings.

It should be noted that these billing codes can be modified for those patients receiving only counseling (psychotherapy) and for others that receive counseling (psychotherapy) and medical evaluation and management services. These evaluation and management services involve a variety of responsibilities unique to the medical management of psychiatric patients such as medical diagnostic evaluation (e.g., evaluation of comorbid medical conditions, drug interactions, and physical examinations), drug management when indicated, physician orders, and interpretation of laboratory or other medical diagnostic studies and observations. Thus, the use of a psychiatric therapeutic billing code with medical evaluation and management services would be appropriate for the clinician who provides both of the key tobacco dependence interventions documented as effective in the guideline: counseling and pharmacotherapy.

In documenting treatment for tobacco dependence using the psychiatric therapeutic procedure codes, the appropriate code is chosen on the basis of the type of psychotherapy (e.g., insight-oriented, behavior modifying, and/or supportive using verbal techniques), the place of service (office vs. inpatient), the face-to-face time spent with the patient during the treatment (both for psychotherapy and medication management), and whether evaluation and management services are furnished on the same date of service as psychotherapy.

B1. Office or Other Outpatient Facility

Insight-oriented, behavior modifying and/or supportive psychotherapy

90804 Individual psychotherapy, insight-oriented, behavior modifying and/or supportive, in an office or outpatient facility, approximately 20 to 30 minutes face-to-face with the patient.

90805 With medical evaluation and management services.

90806 Individual psychotherapy, insight-oriented, behavior modifying and/or supportive, in an office or outpatient facility, approximately 45 to 50 minutes face-to-face with the patient.

90807 With medical evaluation and management services.

90808 Individual psychotherapy, insight-oriented, behavior modifying and/or supportive, in an office or outpatient facility, approximately 75 to 80 minutes face-to-face with the patient.

90809 With medical evaluation and management services.

B2. Inpatient Hospital, Partial Hospital, or Residential Care Facility

Insight-oriented, behavior modifying and/or supportive psychotherapy

90816 Individual psychotherapy, insight-oriented, behavior modifying and/or supportive, in an inpatient hospital, partial hospital, or residential care setting, approximately 20 to 30 minutes face-to-face with the patient.

90817 With medical evaluation and management services.

90818 Individual psychotherapy, insight-oriented, behavior modifying and/or supportive, in an inpatient hospital, partial hospital, or residential care setting, approximately 20 to 30 minutes face-to-face with the patient.

90819 With medical evaluation and management services.

90821 Individual psychotherapy, insight-oriented, behavior modifying and/or supportive, in an inpatient hospital, partial hospital, or residential care setting, approximately 20 to 30 minutes face-to-face with the patient.

90822 With medical evaluation and management services.

B3. Other Psychotherapy

90853 Group psychotherapy (other than a multiple-family group).

B4. Dental Code

01320 Tobacco counseling for the control and prevention of oral disease.

Appendix C: Financial Disclosures for Panel Members, Consultants, and Senior Project Staff

Panel Members

Michael C. Fiore has served as a consultant for, given lectures sponsored by, or has conducted research sponsored by Ciba-Geigy, SmithKline Beecham, Lederle Laboratories, McNeil, Elan Pharmaceutical, and Glaxo Wellcome.

William C. Bailey has served as a consultant for, given lectures sponsored by, or has conducted research sponsored by Glaxo Wellcome, SmithKline Beecham, Schering-Plough, 3M Pharmaceuticals, Pfizer, and Sepracor.

Stuart J. Cohen has not served as a consultant for, given lectures sponsored by, or conducted research sponsored by any pharmaceutical company.

Sally Faith Dorfman has served as a consultant for, given lectures sponsored by, or has conducted research sponsored by various pharmaceutical companies.

Michael G. Goldstein, in addition to being an employee of the Bayer Corporation, has served as a consultant for, given lectures sponsored by, or has conducted research sponsored by Glaxo Wellcome, McNeil, Ciba-Geigy, SmithKline Beecham, Boehringer Ingelheim, Sano Corporation, Dupont Pharmaceuticals, and Eli Lilly.

Ellen R. Gritz has served as a consultant for, given lectures sponsored by, or has conducted research sponsored by Bristol Myers Squibb, SmithKline Beecham, and Glaxo Wellcome.

Richard B. Heyman has not served as a consultant for, given lectures sponsored by, or conducted research sponsored by any pharmaceutical company.

Carlos Roberto Jaén has served as a consultant for, given lectures sponsored by, or has conducted research sponsored by Glaxo Wellcome Pharmaceuticals.

Thomas E. Kottke has served as a consultant for, given lectures sponsored by, or has conducted research sponsored by McNeil Consumer Healthcare.

Harry A. Lando has served as a consultant for, given lectures sponsored by, or has conducted research sponsored by Glaxo Wellcome and SmithKline Beecham.

Robert Mecklenburg has served as a consultant for, given lectures sponsored by, or has conducted research sponsored by SmithKline Beecham and Glaxo Wellcome.

Patricia Dolan Mullen has not served as a consultant for, given lectures sponsored by, or has conducted research sponsored by any pharmaceutical companies.

Louise M. Nett has not served as a consultant for, given lectures sponsored by, or conducted research sponsored by any pharmaceutical company.

Lawrence Robinson has not served as a consultant for, given lectures sponsored by, or conducted research sponsored by any pharmaceutical company.

Maxine L. Stitzer has served as a consultant for, given lectures sponsored by, or has conducted research sponsored by McNeil and SmithKline Beecham.

Anthony C. Tommasello has not served as a consultant for, given lectures sponsored by, or conducted research sponsored by any pharmaceutical company.

Louise Villejo has served as a consultant for, given lectures sponsored by, or has conducted research sponsored by Ortho Biotech.

Mary Ellen Wewers has not served as a consultant for, given lectures sponsored by, or conducted research sponsored by any pharmaceutical company.

Consultants

Timothy Baker has served as a consultant for, given lectures sponsored by, or has conducted research sponsored by Elan Pharmaceutical, SmithKline Beecham, Glaxo Wellcome, and Lederle.

Victor Hasselblad has served as a consultant for, given lectures sponsored by, or has conducted research sponsored by CorTheraputics, Skinceuticals, Merck, Novartis, AstraZeneca, AstraCharnwood, The Medicines, Pfizer, Daiichi, Hoffman-LaRoche, RhonePolenc Rorer, Alexion, SmithKline Beecham, Dade, Quad-C, and Centocor Lilly.

Marc Manley has not served as a consultant for, given lectures sponsored by, or conducted research sponsored by any pharmaceutical company.

David L. Schriger has served as a consultant for, given lectures sponsored by, or has conducted research sponsored by Pfizer Corporation and the MedAmerica Corporation.

David W. Wetter has not served as a consultant for, given lectures sponsored by, or conducted research sponsored by any pharmaceutical company.

Senior Project Staff

Brion J. Fox has not served as a consultant for, given lectures sponsored by, or has conducted research sponsored by any pharmaceutical company.

Index

Guideline Availability

This guideline is available in several formats suitable for health care practitioners, the scientific community, educators, and consumers.

The *Clinical Practice Guideline* presents recommendations for health care providers with brief supporting information, tables and figures, and pertinent references.

The *Quick Reference Guide* is a distilled version of the clinical practice guideline, with summary points for ready reference on a day-to-day basis.

The *Consumer Version* is an information booklet for the general public to increase consumer knowledge and involvement in health care decisionmaking.

The full text of the guideline documents and the meta-analyses references for online retrieval are available by visiting the Surgeon General's Web site at: **www.surgeongeneral.gov/tobacco/default.htm.**

Single copies of these guideline products and further information on the availability of other derivative products can be obtained by calling any of the following Public Health Service organization's toll-free numbers:

Agency for Healthcare Research and Quality (AHRQ)
800-358-9295

Centers for Disease Control and Prevention (CDC)
800-CDC-1311

National Cancer Institute (NCI)
800-4-CANCER

Notes

Notes